The Leadership Code

# THE

PAUL "WHITEY" KAPSALIS
WITH TED GREGORY

# LEADERSHIP
# CODE

## USING LIFE'S
## LESSONS TO
## INSPIRE OTHERS

Meyer & Meyer Sport

British Library Cataloguing in Publication Data
A catalogue record for this book is available from the British Library

**The Leadership Code**
Maidenhead: Meyer & Meyer Sport (UK) Ltd., 2017
ISBN: 978-1-78255-102-7

© 2017 by Meyer & Meyer Sport (UK) Ltd.
Auckland, Beirut, Dubai, Hägendorf, Hong Kong, Indianapolis, Cairo, Cap Town, Manila, Maidenhead, New Delhi, Singapore, Sydney, Teheran, Vienna

Member of the World Sport Publishers' Association (WSPA)
www.w-s-p-a.org

Printed by: C-M Books, Ann Arbor, MI, USA
ISBN: 978-1-78255-102-7
E-Mail: info@m-m-sports.com
www.m-m-sports.com

# ▌CONTENTS

# FOREWORD

In the fall of 2015, I had the great fortune of reconnecting with my long-time friend, Paul "Whitey" Kapsalis, at my son's high school soccer game in Indianapolis. While we were discussing our children, soccer, old times, and life in general, he encouraged me to read his book, *To Chase a Dream*.

I bought it and was so engrossed that I simply could not put it down. I read into the early hours of the morning to finish it. Both of my sons, Matthew and Michael, read the book and were mesmerized and positively affected by its imagery and messages.

Whitey's next book, *The Leadership Code,* is a powerful, entertaining, and honest tale of his lifelong journey of leadership through his story and those of others. It is an inspiring collection of real-life examples of perseverance, resilience, belief, spirituality, commitment, reflection, and growth that Whitey distills into a rock-solid code—one he developed over the years and strives to live by.

At the core of Whitey's belief is that anyone can be a successful leader in any occupation and at any stage or point of their lives. The examples and events he shares have helped him become masterful at helping others to believe, succeed, and, ultimately, lead.

Having spent many years in education as a teacher, coach, and administrator, the lessons learned from *The Leadership Code* most certainly align with my personal beliefs when it comes to leading people. Whitey's story, grounded in the Greek word *philotimo*—pride in humility and placing others first—would empower anyone who reads it to embrace a leadership role wherever he or she is in life or simply inspire them to live more purpose-filled lives. I know this from experience. I've watched Whitey speak to hundreds of young people and adults at my school and have seen the impact of his words.

*The Leadership Code* is told in only the way that Whitey can tell it, which is transparent, engaging, forthright, and with great humility. Anyone who has worked hard and is interested in becoming an inspirational example of an everyday leader will be better for having read Whitey's book. I cannot recommend it strongly enough.

*–John Bertram, Ed.S*

*Principal, Castle North Middle School*

# ■ INTRODUCTION: NO PIE CHARTS, JUST HEART

I've never counted them all, but I bet thousands, maybe tens of thousands, of books have been written about leadership. Many of those have included in-depth, academic studies and research, data, and analysis.

You won't find much of that here.

In these pages, you'll find what I gleaned from a lifetime of ups and downs on my journey to becoming a leader of sorts—and you'll find similar observations from the stories of others I like to call exceptional everyday leaders. You may have heard of some; you've probably never heard of others. The common bond between them is they navigated their way to becoming leaders.

Like me, they grew into leaders through challenges and through trial and error; in other words, through getting their hands dirty. They, and I, saw examples in other people. Maybe they were fortunate enough to have mentors, as I was. Maybe they had to figure all of it out on their own. Whatever the individual situations and stories, we learned lessons and developed practices, approaches, and philosophies over time that worked, and we ditched those that didn't.

The other common bond is that we have heart. We understand that leadership starts there and is inspired by genuinely caring for others.

I'm Greek American, and in my family we like to refer to a Greek word that has a lot to do with heart: *philotimo*. My mom displays it on a little plaque, along with a quote from Philippians 2:3-4, in her kitchen, one of my favorite places on earth. I'll explain more about *philotimo* later.

For now, I'll just say that *philotimo* roughly translates to honor in doing the right thing. I take that concept very, very seriously, as do the other people you'll read about in this book.

The result is something like a mosaic that came together over the decades of my life and the lives of others who tell their stories in the pages that follow. From that mosaic I've created what I might call my leadership code—a general approach to life that mentors and inspires others.

Some of you picking up this book may think it's irrelevant because you're not in a leadership position, not in the conventional sense. Or maybe you think you're too young to consider yourself a leader, or too old, or have been in a low-level career slot for decades.

But one of the fundamental messages I want to convey here is that you don't have to be in a leadership position to be a leader. Leaders exist across all levels of our society and culture—not just CEOs or presidents or senior vice presidents or deans or superintendents or captains of your sports team or generals or other managers and administrators. Leaders can be sitting right next to you, maybe performing a role that wouldn't generally be associated with leadership. Doesn't matter where you are. You can still be a leader, and you can lead every day in small and large ways.

It actually begins much earlier than whatever exterior position you may attain in life. The onset of leadership begins with a commitment to yourself—a commitment to make good choices, to build healthy relationships, to be accountable to others, to care enough about what you are doing to make a positive impact and to leave a lasting and sustainable influence on the things you touch. To improve the culture.

You don't have to be a general to do that.

It's commonly known that in an airplane, if the oxygen masks drop down from the overhead compartment, the adults are instructed to put the masks on themselves, then place the masks on their children. The notion of making sure you're healthy and safe before you can help others is the same for leadership. It means making the decision to take responsibility, and it takes grooming, some molding, some luck, and time. But first, you must be committed to leadership within yourself.

See, I believe a great leader is not chosen randomly. I believe a great leader chooses to lead and earns his or her way to that place over a period of time through respect for and from others. A great leader cares more about overall results than about individual success. A great leader leads from the heart with compassion, trust, and respect for those around him or her. A great leader is someone who left a place or situation better than the way he or she found it.

In the following pages, I'll explore and explain some of the different places in life where leadership presents itself and how all of us can seize those chances to make the world a better place in small, medium, and large ways. I'll do that by sharing my story and allowing others to share their stories.

You'll read about leadership in a family, leadership in sports, leadership in fatherhood, leadership in your community, and leadership in friendship. In each of those instances, I'll emphasize that it doesn't matter what place you occupy. What matters is how you occupy that place.

And, I promise to keep it simple and practical. I don't want this to be a massive tome that's intimidating and overwhelming – one of those books you think you should and would read, but that you never will. Above all else, I've tried to make this accessible – something you could carry with you easily in a briefcase, backpack, carry-on bag, or whatever your preferred electronic device is.

No charts, graphs, data, diagrams, or dense scientific analysis that only management researchers or MBA candidates might find engaging. This is for everybody of all ages, even management researchers and MBA candidates.

These are real stories of people much like you, people with a lot of heart, who grew into leaders and absorbed lessons that I think you might find helpful wherever you are on your leadership journey and from whatever place you choose to lead.

In the end, I hope to accomplish my goals of giving you steps you can apply right now and giving you some things to ponder about why we lead the way we do. I hope you enjoy it.

I've thoroughly enjoyed the adventure getting here and will enjoy wherever the path may lead.

*–Paul "Whitey" Kapsalis*

# ■ CHAPTER 1
# LIVING A PHILOTIMO LIFE

## ■ LEADERSHIP IN THE FAMILY

Growing up, our family moved around quite a bit. My dad worked in the insurance industry, and every time he'd earn a promotion, we'd pack up and head to the next town. My parents started their family in Chicago. Then we moved to Rockford, Illinois; Collinsville, Illinois; Edina, Minnesota; Southfield, Michigan; and finally to Carmel, Indiana, a suburb of Indianapolis. All those places by the time I was 15 years old.

It could be a little tough, moving that much, but one of the positive results was that my siblings—three brothers and one sister—and I became a pretty tight group. We're fairly close in age, which probably made it a little easier. And, over time, we became leaders—something that I think happened without us really knowing it most of the time.

That's because our parents, Andy and Becky Kapsalis, knew how to instill those qualities largely through the examples they set each and every day. All of us kids picked up on that and are eternally grateful for what they gave us.

As a parent, leadership obviously is crucial to the health, or illness, of a family. Whether they know it or not, parents are leaders. My parents, and probably every parent out there, understand that concept to some degree. What parents say—and more importantly what they do—creates the foundation and more for their children, who then will go into the world and make an impact on other lives.

I believe a misconception exists out there that parents, especially fathers, need to be almost like dictators to their children, telling them what they should do, how they should behave, what they should become, and how they should go about their journey.

I think parenting may be a lot simpler than that. More important than dictating is demonstrating genuine care and love, listening, supporting, being accessible and all-inclusive, and being present in the moment with your kids.

One of my favorite characteristics of those is listening, more specifically engaged listing. It's a great tool in building togetherness. If you actively listen to your children, I bet you'll find that they are pretty intuitive and aware when given the chance to talk.

The other misconception that I believe is out there is that many parents—again, especially fathers—feel they need to appear invincible to their children, that they never have doubts, fears, or struggles. While dads absolutely must try to be the rock within the family structure, I am a strong believer that this strength can be demonstrated in good times and in challenging times by being transparent with our children in small, appropriate doses. That can be a very powerful leadership and family-building tool. I will delve more into the magic of that characteristic in a later chapter.

I want to be clear here: I'm not saying parents should let kids do what they want. They need to lay down the law when they need to lay down the law. Children want and need boundaries, need to be corrected, need to understand what's right and wrong, and need to appreciate that consequences exist for their actions. I simply believe that the less heavy-handed a parent can be—the more he or she looks for ways to be a guide rather than a dictator—the stronger the relationship with their children will be and the more likely those children will grow into healthy, purposeful adults who contribute to their community in uplifting ways. We need to help get them where they want to go, not necessarily where we think they should go.

In our family growing up, I think it started with the Greek word I mentioned in the introduction: *philotimo*, that honor in doing the right thing. But *philotimo* has a much broader definition that and, like a lot of words from foreign languages, doesn't have an exact translation to English. It encompasses honor in self, honor in family, and honor in community. It's not an ego-driven honor—although a certain level of quiet confidence is an integral part of it.

On a small board right next to the window in my parents' kitchen is probably the most complete explanation of *philotimo*. Written on what looks like a chalkboard that school kids more than a century ago might have used, my mom placed right under the word an excerpt from Philippians 2: 3-4: "Do nothing out of selfish ambition or vain conceit. Rather, in humility value others above yourselves, not looking to your own interests but each of you to the interests of others."

I love that quote, and I think it gives maybe the richest English translation of *philotimo*.

The word conveys a strong sense of right, wrong, and unselfishness. If you wanted to distill *philotimo* to one word, I guess that might be "heart."

That was the atmosphere we were raised in. And the physical "heart of the heart" was our kitchen table. In my family, so much happened around that kitchen table. It's where we ate, where we talked, where we laughed, where we cried, and, most importantly, where we gathered and shared. I am so grateful for the kitchen table.

It is a bit of a lost art, but my wife and I still try to make the kitchen table in our house the center of all activity and communication among us. We don't always get to eat and sit at the kitchen table as a family, but when we do we certainly maximize the opportunity. In fact, our kitchen table is my mom and dad's old kitchen table, so the memories and stories continue to get passed on as a legacy of our family.

My parents always were accessible at their kitchen table, and while we shared so many terrific meals over the course of my lifetime at that table, the real benefit was the togetherness that we shared.

From our earliest years and through all our moves from city to city, we kids have memories of that kitchen table and of my parents doing a handful of things to foster that atmosphere of togetherness and sharing.

First, as I referred to earlier, they always looked to promote that concept of us as one tight unit, and we loved it because our parents genuinely enjoyed, even cherished, the notion of us all being together as one. They both come from very close, immigrant families—households that always had an open door and drew people to them, which I think strengthened the bond in their nuclear families.

That immigrant experience—one of the enduring components that makes our country so great—had another element for us. Our parents made us very aware of our roots and our grandparents' journeys from the villages of Greece. As teenagers in the early 1900s, our *Papous* and *Yiayias*—grandfathers and grandmothers—summoned an enormous amount of courage, left remote regions of Greece where they'd barely heard about the United States of America, and traveled over the Atlantic Ocean "on the boat," as they say. After they arrived, they connected with relatives or acquaintances, somehow carved out a life from virtually nothing, raised families, made it through the Great Depression, suffered their share of heartbreak, and laid a foundation for all of us to follow. They accomplished all that while barely being able to speak English.

It gets me choked up every time I think very long about their inner strength and commitment to make a better life—for themselves, yes, but most important, for their sons and daughters and grandchildren, all those who came after them. Talk about courage and sacrifice and *philotimo*.

All these decades later, their journeys remain a source of eternal appreciation and inspiration for me and my siblings to hunker down and move forward, to make our *Papous* and *Yiayias* proud of what they started, what they gave us. I guess I could call it *philotimo forward*.

My mom and dad understood how important that foundation was by making sure we spent as much time as possible with our grandparents. And, whether or not we could be with my grandparents, my folks shared stories about them with us.

Like the homes where my parents grew up—actually, they were tiny apartments on the north side of Chicago—our houses always had an open door. It was a place where all our friends and our parents' friends liked to hang out. At the heart of all that was the seven of us: Andy, Becky, Pete, Danny, Paul, Deanne, and Dino—plus a few dogs along the way.

We often had great, big, loud parties filled with laughter and music and stories. At times, I'm sure it was overwhelming for some visitors, but they never forgot those gatherings and the atmosphere created, and most of them—the fun ones—always wanted to come back.

Another crucial thing my parents did to create that core strong family, which became one of the foundational tiles in the mosaic of leadership, revolved around our activities. All of us were graced with my parents' athletic skills, and we loved sports. My dad and mom used sports to acclimate us to a new community quickly. It was a way for us to fit in and make friends fast. Our participation in sports and our capacities to hold our own against just about anybody gave us instant credibility with other kids. It also created in us a quiet confidence in new situations. We could be shy but not necessarily socially awkward in front of others, whether they were kids our age or adults.

Today, my parents will say that one of the things they stressed in raising us was giving us that inner, quiet confidence, and I think their conscious effort to do that through sports and in other ways worked, if you don't mind me displaying some of that quiet confidence in saying that.

Another way our parents worked toward that was by placing a high priority on all of us supporting each other at our games or other activities. If one of us had a soccer or hockey game or a dance performance or a figure skating competition, all of us piled in the van and drove there to cheer. Our parents' enthusiasm for doing that kind of thing was sincere and infectious. We caught on, never complained, and always looked forward to those outings.

And, they never compared one kid with another, nor did we do that with each other. If Pete had a hockey game and scored three goals, and I had a game a few hours later and got skunked, my parents wouldn't note the difference. Instead, they celebrated Pete's hat trick, which prompted us to celebrate it, too. And, you know what? It felt much better to celebrate Pete's great performance than it did to wallow in my own pity.

We also had unspoken expectations. None of us really got to see my dad compete in baseball and basketball, two sports he excelled in. But in our houses the various trophies and awards he'd won over the years were displayed here and there. That was almost enough motivation for us kids, but both our parents supplemented that by encouraging us to be the best we could be. They made it clear that each of us could reach high achievements in whatever endeavor we were pursuing if we kept working hard and kept our enthusiasm levels high. The key concept here is encouragement.

All of us boys have done at least a little coaching—some of us a lot of coaching—and what we see too often is parents pushing, pushing, pushing their kids relentlessly in one direction. After a while, that pushing just causes many kids to implode, burn out, and hate an activity he or she started out loving.

We never had that. Our dad was a baseball and basketball guy growing up and through his twenties and thirties. Our mom was a cheerleader. We boys became primarily soccer players, but we also played quite a bit of hockey. Deanne was a dancer and ice skater.

They never pushed us to do those things that they were most familiar with and always encouraged us to do whatever it was we wanted, as long as we stayed active. My dad knew nothing about soccer. In fact, he used to make fun of soccer players when he was growing up. But, when he saw our interest start cooking, he realized what a wonderful team game it was and what valuable lessons it could teach about working together and discipline, among other things. He shifted gears and, right from the get-go, supported us 200 percent, as did my mom, who also knew next to nothing about the sport. In fact, in pretty short order they became true aficionados of the game. It's an example not only of selflessness but also of allowing a kid to determine his or her own path—an early precursor to becoming a leader.

I had a pretty ideal childhood, but that doesn't mean that we were always locking arms and singing *Kumbayah* while we strolled through our days and nights. As close and supportive as we are, we also can be very competitive with each other. We had our scuffles and scrapes. Imagine being Deanne, the one daughter tossed in with four spirited boys. We could be pretty rough on her. But, even in that competition, we created a sort of camaraderie among us kids.

If Danny and Pete, for example, got into an argument, our parents sometimes would let them fight it out, and most times, we turned out to be bluffing. My dad remembers more than a few occasions when Pete and Danny would start to tangle and my dad would say, "Okay, you know, I'd love to see a great fight. Let's go out in the backyard so you don't crack an elbow on the corner of the counter or break a chair."

Pete and Danny suddenly would fall silent, look at each other, and say, "Well, we don't really want to fight each other," and the anger would just melt away.

My mom recalls the very first time she and my dad enlisted Pete to babysit for all of us. He was 11 years old, and my parents were only going across the street to a neighbor's house for the evening.

"We were a nervous wreck. I thought, 'Oh my gosh, they're probably going to kill each other,'" my mom told me. "When we came home, there was a note and it read, 'Mom, we broke a glass, and I had to pick it up.' So, the next morning I was complimenting him, saying, 'Gee, Pete, you did a good job.' He says, 'What do you think? We're going to fight when you're not around to break it up?'" My mom started laughing. "He's eleven years old, and I thought, 'Who's the adult here?'"

Then, there were the times that we'd be playing in the backyard—I couldn't tell you how many thousands of hours we played together in our backyards throughout the Midwest—and a fight actually would break out between us. Or we'd get into some other kind of trouble. My mom would come storming out of the house angry at us and ready to inflict her own punishment. The sight of her charging out the backdoor—sometimes armed with a hockey stick—would get us to stop immediately. Pete would sound the call for all of us to beat a hasty retreat. Faster than you could say "Pele," we'd run out the backyard to the park or any other refuge safe from our mom's wrath, laughing all the way, or at least most of the way, once the fear subsided. So, Pete demonstrated early leadership skills in that sense.

My parents also wouldn't lie to us. If we had a bad game or performance or a poor grade in school, they wouldn't confuse us by insisting we'd done well. They'd be silent, which was really the best approach because that let us process what had happened and not be judged. In that way and in many others, they let us be us, and each of us developed our own distinct personality, another tile at the base of the mosaic that led to a leadership code. But the common theme—the thing that our parents stressed and lived in their own lives—was our kindness and unconditional support for our siblings and for others.

Through all those experiences, we learned that in any of our roles we could be leaders, not in the conventional sense where we constantly were barking orders to the others. That would have created chaos. It was more like we had a shared set of values and perspectives so that, in any given set of circumstances, one or all of us could provide an example of leadership.

It started when we were squirts on the soccer field. One of the funnier pictures we have in our collection of thousands of family photos is of Danny and me surrounding little Dino—I think he was about four years old, maybe three feet tall—on the sidelines at halftime of his game. We'd pulled him aside and while the other kids on his team were enjoying snacks, Danny and I were talking intently to him, an eight-year-old and six-year-old giving coaching tips to their little brother. Poor Dino. The photo shows him staring into space, a lost, overwhelmed expression on his face.

Oh well, whatever we were telling him came from our hearts; pint-size *philotimo* on display.

It's a little tricky, I'll admit, to think of being a leader as a child in a family. What if, as in my case and in Danny's, Deanne's, and Dino's cases, you have older siblings? How can it be possible to lead if you're five years old and your older brother is 12? Heck, how can a 12-year-old be considered a leader?

Leadership as a child begins with the decision to be responsible to others within your family, regardless if you are an only child or if you come from a large family, and being a good son or daughter to your parents.

Most importantly you must be transparent. I'm the father of three, and let me tell you, the most difficult thing for me to gauge, and I believe it's true for many parents, is how our children are feeling. By "feeling," I don't mean physically as much as I mean my children's emotional and mental health. I want to know how they really are feeling. What their fears are. What their dreams are. What their possibilities and limitations are. Even who their friends are and what makes those friends special.

Being open and honest about all these scenarios within your family can be extremely tough and uncomfortable as a kid. But it is crucial. It builds a trust and bond that will last a lifetime. It builds a strong relationship in that family and in that home, and that strength builds confidence and leadership qualities outside the home. While growing up in my family, I learned that nothing is more powerful than the unyielding support from that family.

As a parent, it's important to show your children that it is their responsibility, and a great opportunity, to build that trusted relationship by sharing their feelings, by not being afraid to show their emotions, by trusting that those around them can help them get to where they ultimately want to be, and, by being engaged with others in their own fears and struggles and triumphs. The child's genuine interest in the well-being and support of his or her parents and siblings is as important as sharing his or her own feelings. It's a healthy exchange that creates that strong relationship I'm talking about here. Showing their parents and siblings that they care is a great form of leadership and will allow them to be a resource to all family members for life. By the way, parents have their own responsibilities when it comes to sharing. We'll get into that later.

That lifelong bond begins with a choice to be a leader wherever you fall in the family lineup—oldest to youngest. I'm smack dab in the middle of my siblings, third oldest of five. At some point, I guess I must have made a conscious choice to be a leader of my emotions, a leader of my contributions, a leader of my love and commitment to the group, above and beyond my own individual goals and objectives. I'm so glad that I did and that my brothers and sister did, that we followed the lead of our parents. When this type of leadership exists in the home, it translates outward into everyday life. It's no coincidence that each of us were captains of our respective teams growing up, as far back as I can recall, and I remember the sense of responsibility and privilege of wearing the "C" on the jersey. I like to think we lead as captains of our teams in the same way that we lead within the walls of our home.

And, while I'm at it, let me point out that the examples my parents set went beyond our immediate family. Wherever we landed on our moves throughout the Midwest, my parents almost immediately assessed the situation in the community, went out, got involved, and initiated changes that made our corner of the universe—and often conditions beyond our corner—better places. Many times they faced fairly strong opposition to what they wanted to do.

My mom was president of the women's group at our church in Rockford, Illinois, and my dad was parish treasurer. They created soccer leagues in Minnesota and Michigan when we moved to those states. They spearheaded the push to make soccer a high school-sanctioned varsity sport when we moved to Indiana. That also was where, after realizing that quality soccer shoes, shin guards, and other gear were virtually nonexistent in local stores, my parents started a soccer retail outlet that became one of the most successful enterprises of its kind in the nation and was named by US Soccer as the Best Soccer Store in the Country. Through that enterprise, Soccer Unlimited, we created soccer camps that about 20,000 kids attended over the years. It was a great instrument for us to pay it forward and to positively influence young boys and girls, using soccer as the tool. Our leadership responsibilities were never measured by the platform. In other words, we did not have to be on a grand stage to know that we could make a difference. Whether we had 12 kids attend a camp or 500 kids attend a camp, we approached them all from a training and leadership perspective with the same passion and desire that lived inside of us.

And, my parents always shared the lessons learned and expertise gained with others who wanted to do the same things—another important element of true leadership that some are reluctant to do. Their leadership style played itself out among us kids at fairly early ages.

We had a chance to resurrect a lot of those moments on Father's Day in 2016 when my mom had the five of us for breakfast. We sat around the kitchen table talking about our family dynamic as we were growing up, something all of us together had never really done before, at least not in this type of "formal" setting. Through all the stories and laughter, a few remembrances really stayed with me.

Like the time when I was 9 years old and playing soccer on a team with other 9-year-olds in the Minneapolis area. We were a pretty strong team. My coach at the time, a wonderful guy named Dale Grauze, would allow my brother Pete, who was 13 back then, to act as a sort of unofficial assistant coach at practices. Pete would later go on to be an extremely successful coach, and Dale must have sensed that even as a 13-year-old this kid had some serious soccer acumen, because Dale let Pete coach us for a game, and not just any game. It was the league championship.

It happened when, at the last minute, Dale was called out of town on business the weekend of our big game. Without blinking an eye, he turned over the reins to Pete. He had all the confidence in the world in this boy who was barely a teenager, or at least Dale demonstrated that he did. Who knew what he really thought? Either way, I've always viewed that move as an intriguing example of leadership.

Dale informed the parents, who were livid and protested. But he stuck to his decision. And, when Pete stood on the sidelines leading our team a few days later, a couple of dads took it upon themselves to critique every move he made quite audibly while standing a few feet directly behind Pete.

Essentially, they screamed at him the whole time. And, Pete stood there and took it, never wavering in the approach and strategies he'd learned by working with us for the entire season and playing the game for years.

Looking back now, I had to believe that a fairly big chunk of the confidence he displayed had emanated from seeing my parents wade into new and sometimes hostile territory and calmly go about the business of doing what's right and best for all. Even by that young age, Pete had been fortified by the support he'd received from our parents and his siblings. He probably didn't fully grasp all that, but to this day, I'm pretty amazed he handled it with such poise.

By the way, we ended up winning the championship by a score of something like 5-2. Afterward, those two dads who'd yelled at Pete most of the game approached him to apologize. Here's hoping they learned a lesson or two about leadership that day.

Another example that we recalled sitting around the table that Father's Day morning had to do with my brother Danny, who also was a terrific soccer player.

In the late 1970s, he was 15 years old and had dreamed for a few years of playing professional soccer. The North American Soccer League, a fledgling professional enterprise trying to bring soccer to the US sporting masses, announced that a team was headed to Detroit. We lived in suburban Detroit at the time, and Danny wanted to try out.

Even then, he was a technically gifted soccer player. Years later Danny would decide to try out and earn a spot on powerhouse Indiana University's soccer team. He ended up being a part of one of IU's national championship teams.

But he had about as much of a chance of landing a spot on the Detroit Express back then as he had of being elected president of the United States. Zero.

I'd be willing to bet that the vast majority of parents and siblings would have leveled with Danny and spared him the embarrassment, or spared themselves the hassle of schlepping a kid to a tryout for a team he had no chance of making.

Our family did the exact opposite. His brothers and sister encouraged him and tried to get him ready for what to expect. And, my parents decided to let him give it his best shot.

"That's part of instilling confidence," my dad said that morning. "Danny was 15 years old. All these guys were in their 20s; some might have been 28 years old, and this little kid who maybe comes up to their shoulder is mixing it up with them in drills, and he didn't blink an eye.

"We knew he wasn't going to make the team, but that wasn't our purpose," my dad continued. "Our purpose was that he had a thought in his mind, and we said, 'Go for it. If nothing else, it'll be a great learning experience for him,' and it did turn out to be a great experience for him."

He was never given serious consideration to make the team, which was the correct decision. But, the other players gave the little guy a standing ovation when he walked from the field. And, a newspaper reporter covering the tryout was beguiled by Danny's moxie. The next day's issue of the *Detroit Free Press* had a story and photo of little Danny Kapsalis trying out for the Detroit Express.

That anecdote has a couple of elements that really appeal to me. One is my parents saying why not give it a shot and the other is Danny's guts in going ahead and showing up at that field. He had to be the youngest guy by about eight years. He was maybe 5 feet, 5 inches tall and 110 pounds. That level of gumption to try out bordered on oblivious ignorance.

"No," my dad said when I pointed that out. "He had confidence."

To this day, Danny says the experience gave him the confidence to try out at Indiana University several years later.

In those childhood years, Dino and Deanne had been a little overwhelmed and overrun by we three older siblings. They'd become especially close when my parents opened Soccer Unlimited in 1982. Dino was a fifth grader; Deanne was a couple of years older.

Our parents were gone quite a bit. Pete was playing soccer at Michigan State and Danny, and I were busy with high school soccer and activities. For about five years there, it was just Deanne and Dino. She'd be waiting for him when he came home from school and did it all for him. Dino remembered her as "my best friend and my mom."

That time was exceptional for Dino and Deanne, but the truth is our closeness carried over into adulthood, and one of the beautiful aspects of it was that each of us didn't have one person who we always went to or one sibling we mentored. All of us took on that role with all the others at one time or another. It's nothing that we take for granted, but it always seems to be there.

I can remember, for example, being a little nervous when our first child, Katrina, started kindergarten a few years ago. I was experiencing Monday morning anxiety and turned to Pete, already a father with kids in school. We talked and listened and within a few minutes, he gave me such a sense of peace that everything was going to work out just fine.

We all went on to succeed as leaders in a few different ways. Pete won three state championships as an Indiana high school soccer coach and then went into college coaching. Danny took over for Pete at the same high school and won another state championship. I ended up as captain of Indiana University's soccer team and years later established a golf outing that has raised more than a half million dollars for pancreatic cancer research. Dino joined me in leading Soccer Unlimited for a few years. Most recently, Deanne developed SoulCore, a hugely popular meditative experience that pairs core strengthening, stretching, and functional movement with the prayers of the rosary.

And, we all stayed close. To this day, the five of us, along with our 19 children, live within a half hour of each other and our parents in the Indianapolis area. I like that. We all do.

We were wrapping up our breakfast visit on that Father's Day at my parents' house when we finally got around to asking Dino what he thought about all this. As the youngest, he was in a fortunate position in some ways. He had the benefit of observing and learning from the successes and failures, trials and tribulations of the siblings who came before him.

"I'll answer that this way," Dino said. "My definition of leadership really involves three things: One, a leader gives people something to belong to. Two, a leader will provide a clear direction or clear vision, and three, that leader will inspire to bring out the best."

He remembered that seeing his big brothers and sister excel in their activities and give strong support to each other drove him to do well, a drive that was helped by the strong competitive streak that runs through all of us. He had a passion for soccer from the time he could walk, and he also became a really strong high school and college player.

And, he talked about how Pete, after finishing his playing career at Michigan State and graduating, returned home to help run Soccer Unlimited.

"When Pete came home, I don't know if he saw potential in me or not, but he really pulled a lot out of me in terms of what I could become and instilled a lot of belief," Dino said while we sat around the table.

"Danny did the same thing. Then, as I left high school, Whitey became that person for me, saying, 'Okay, here's what it takes to get to this level.' It was huge. Those impacts were tremendous.

"I guess my point," Dino said, "is that I felt a sense of belonging. I had a clear sense of direction, and I was inspired."

Well, I guess we passed Dino's criteria of leadership.

But, it was his last observation that stayed with me the longest after we left my parents' table that morning. It had to do with his final soccer game at Indiana University. IU lost in the quarterfinals of the post-season and Dino's career, which began 20 years earlier when he started walking and kicking a soccer ball before he could form a full sentence, was over in the blink of an eye.

It was a pretty jarring realization, made even more painful by the fact that the team lost the game at home in Bloomington in front of a big crowd.

"I remember going back to my apartment after the game, and I was like, 'This is crazy,'" Dino said. "I'm just sitting in my room. The team had plans to have a party after the game—win or lose—at our place."

All of us—except for Deanne, who was working and living in Chicago at the time—were at the game, my parents included. After we connected with Dino and went out to dinner, we were getting ready to head home and let Dino get to his party.

"It was a pretty tough moment for me," Dino recalled, "and you recognized it."

We were standing there for a few awkward moments, none of us really knowing how to say goodbye to Dino. Our hearts were aching for him, sensing he was a kind of unsteady and just plain sad.

I spoke first, but Pete and Danny were thinking the same thing I was.

"You know what?" I said. "I think I'm going to stay."

"Yeah," Pete said, "I can stay, too."

"I'm in," Danny said.

All three of us accompanied Dean and his teammates at the party, and we all spent the night.

More than two decades later, Dino remembered that gesture from his three big brothers.

"We had a great night," he said at our Father's Day breakfast. "It took all the pain away, and I knew life was going to be good. Everything was going to be fine. That's what it did for me."

He said soccer was great for all four of us and our parents, even Deanne.

"I mean, we had incredible experiences and opportunities as a result," Dino said. "But that bond right there, that night, was probably the most meaningful moment of my entire career."

I had no idea, nor did Pete or Danny, I think, that it meant so much to Dino. It was just kind of a natural response that we'd developed over the years. It wasn't that the party was the greatest party ever. It merely was us just wanting to spend time with Dino at this sad moment in his personal journey. Leadership isn't always about talking. Sometimes leadership is simply about being present.

It was a leadership response that may not have looked like one and may not have fit the conventional profile of a leader, but a leader in the context of *philotimo*, of leading with the heart.

# ■ CHAPTER 2
# PURSUIT OF THE DREAM

## ■ LEADERSHIP IN SPORTS

By this time, you know that soccer was a central activity in my life and the lives of my immediate family. But that activity grew to become something so much more: a rich foundation for many life lessons and lessons in leadership. And, it came about almost by accident.

When we were really little, baseball looked like it was going to be our family sport. My dad loved it; he played it growing up and is an intense Chicago Cubs fan, a status that has finally stopped being so miserable and actually has turned quite joyful the last few years.

He got another promotion, and we moved from Rockford, Illinois, in the far northern part of the state, to Collinsville, in southwestern Illinois, near St. Louis. We learned right away that the St. Louis region is a soccer hotbed. Even back then, in the late 1960s, before soccer caught fire as a youth sport across the US, St. Louis kids, teens, and adults played a lot of soccer and really loved it.

We knew nothing about it.

But, like I mentioned earlier, one of the things my parents emphasized when we moved to a new community was sports. It was our path toward getting acclimated fairly quickly to a potential friend base and, generally, to the community.

Pretty quickly after moving to Collinsville, my dad went to a park where youth sports volunteers had set up tables. He asked what sports were available. One of the volunteers said soccer, and my dad asked what else?

There was nothing else, really, not at that moment. It was fall. Baseball season was at least six months away. So, my dad did some quick thinking on his feet, realized that soccer was a team sport, and signed us up, even though he and we knew nothing about the game.

Looking back, it was a pretty smart move.

My mom went out immediately and bought a soccer ball, which we inflated and tossed in the back yard. Then we took to just kicking the thing around and pounding the snot out of each other. After all, we're siblings. Using cones and t-shirts, tree limbs, and whatever else we could find, we set up a makeshift soccer pitch and kept playing and playing and playing.

I fell in love with soccer right away, as did my brothers, and wanted to play all the time; I wanted to absorb everything I could about the game. I guess it doesn't take too much insight to understand why.

It's a game that requires an enormous amount of energy and stamina, which the five of us had a lot of. It's played outdoors, and we loved being outside. It resonates with my love of competition. It requires teamwork, power, grace, athleticism, and footwork. All of us, by the way, love to dance, and I don't mind saying that we're pretty decent on the floor.

At five years old, I made a local all-star team, and we got a chance to play in Busch Stadium where the professional team, the St. Louis Stars, played its games. Before a Stars match, we pint-sized all-stars trekked out to the field and played to a 1-1 tie. It didn't matter that few people were paying attention or that the game ended in a tie. I was hooked on soccer and knew in my heart that I was going to chase that ball for as long as I could.

It was at this point that I inherited my nickname. While my entire family has olive skin and jet-black hair, I came into the world as a tow-head. As a result, my dad, who grew up with nicknames for everyone in his old neighborhood, began calling me "Whitey." The name has stuck with me to this day.

A couple of years later, we moved again, this time to Edina, Minnesota, a wonderful community except for one thing: It had no youth soccer league. So, my parents created the Edina Soccer Association and started with 16 teams. We kept playing, developing our skills and our love for the sport.

Four years after that, we pulled up stakes and moved to Birmingham, Michigan, near Detroit, which did have a youth soccer league. But we arrived in winter and that was hockey season, which wouldn't have been a big deal. We'd been playing a lot of hockey in Minnesota and grew to love that sport, too.

Birmingham's youth hockey season had started a few weeks before we hit town. My dad was able to get us on the rosters of teams, but I wasn't too crazy about playing. I felt like a true outsider, like I was invading this team that had already formed around a bunch of guys who didn't know me and probably didn't want to. On top of everything else, I was on a team of players who were a year or two older than me, and I was already undersized.

When it came time for my first game, I put on the gear, laced up my skates, and then lost my nerve. I told my dad, who was there helping me, that I didn't want to play; I didn't even want to sit on the bench. I was too intimidated. After a little pep talk—in which he told me to just give it this one shot, that if I didn't like it after, I could hang up the skates—I reluctantly trudged to the bench.

The first few minutes were pretty awful, but the entire episode turned out to be a great leadership lesson that at the time I had no idea was occurring. While the game progressed, I sat on the end of the bench, trying to ignore the muttering emanating from the other players on my team. I was miserable and a little scared.

But, when I got on the ice, my instincts and love of the game took over. Or, maybe I channeled my anxiety into energy. Whatever the reason, I played pretty well from the time my skates hit the ice. A couple of minutes later, I scored.

From that moment on, I became our team's secret weapon, and the guys rallied around me like I was their little brother. My mom tells me that was probably the earliest example of me bringing people together—maybe my first unwitting leadership moment. I'll take her word on that.

I do recall learning another leadership lesson that can be applied to the broader journey of life: Confront your fears. I'm so grateful that my dad gave me that little nudge to play. Afterward, I realized I could handle more than I thought I could and that my fears were not all that scary once I went toe to toe with them and embraced the challenge. It strengthened my quiet confidence, which was another fortunate turn in my journey toward leadership and in living a fuller life.

As much as I enjoyed hockey, my love for soccer grew stronger and stronger in me. My brothers and I, and sometimes Deanne, played every single day in our backyard or at a local park. When the Detroit Express came to town, even though the coaches had the nerve to cut Danny, we became passionate fans and went to every home game in the old Pontiac Silverdome. We loved it.

That's when, in the late 1970s, my parents decided to establish another youth soccer league, this one in conjunction with the Express and set up for players who were a little more serious about the game. The Bonanza Express Soccer League created teams in each of the six counties that would play each other. The Detroit Express assigned a player to every team and that player would conduct clinics.

Birmingham also was where Pete blazed another trail for the family, again giving his younger siblings a leadership example. He earned a soccer scholarship to Michigan State University and all of us brothers dreamed that we could do the same thing. I made up my mind that I was going to become a star at Groves High School and follow him to Michigan State.

Our family had other plans.

My dad got another promotion, this time to Indianapolis, and I was pretty angry about it. My life in Birmingham was wonderful, as was Danny's. He was a star on Groves' highly competitive varsity. I had a great group of friends, a nice girlfriend, and a solid plan in place for my future.

I fought my parents the whole way, even threatening to stay with a friend's family for my final three years of high school—a preposterous notion. They wouldn't budge, which was the correct decision. In June 1981 we moved to Carmel, Indiana, a suburb of Indianapolis. We had to start all over again.

Danny detected one spark of hope in that move. He noticed that Indiana University was about 75 miles south of Carmel. All of us boys remembered that IU was where one of our Detroit Express idols, Dave Shelton, played. We knew something else about Indiana University men's soccer team: It was a powerhouse.

As of this writing, IU has won eight national championships in men's soccer. The team is to college soccer what University of Kansas or Duke University is to college basketball; what Ohio State University or University of Alabama is to college football. Indiana's soccer team is expected to contend for a championship virtually every single year.

Back then, the tradition was getting started. Coach Jerry Yeagley took a club team when he arrived in Bloomington in 1963 and, despite opposition from athletic department administrators, transformed it to a varsity sport a decade later.

By 1976, he'd coached Indiana University's team to the NCAA championship game, an achievement repeated in 1978 and 1980 before Indiana won the whole enchilada in 1982 and 1983. Over time, Indiana would win nearly 80 percent of its games, make it to the title game a mind-blowing 14 times, compete in the soccer version of the Final Four known as the College Cup 18 times, and win 12 Big Ten titles.

Danny had dreamed of playing at Indiana and saw our move as taking him one step closer to that dream. I had the exact opposite perception. Moving to Indiana was taking me farther away from everything I'd set my sights on.

But, maybe in another example of how leadership is learned, all of us rallied, faced adverse conditions, and proved ourselves again on the soccer field and in a new community. In his senior year, Danny played like his cleats were on fire, setting the Carmel High School record for goals scored in a single season and leading the Greyhounds all the way to regional finals.

But, he didn't get the attention he had hoped for from college coaches, most notably from Indiana Coach Yeagley. Danny being Danny, he enrolled at IU anyway, trained and tried out for the soccer team, but was cut. All of us were heartbroken for Danny, and that setback underscored the level of play at IU.

Meanwhile, I settled in at Carmel High School and was starting to play pretty well. My junior year, we got to the semi-finals of the state championship, and I was named Best Defensive Player of the tournament, an award handed to me by Coach Yeagley. It was a pretty big deal just to meet him for five seconds.

The next year, we lost in the state championship game and finished runner-up. I had another strong season, strong enough that Michigan State offered me a partial scholarship to play there. I was thrilled. At the same time, Danny showed his resilience and perseverance—a couple of fundamental leadership traits—and kept training. He tried out again for Indiana's team and made it this time. We were absolutely crazy with joy.

That year, Danny worked his way up the roster and saw playing time, the same year IU went on to win a national championship. We have wonderful memories of driving down to Bloomington for games and hanging out a bit with the team. I started to appreciate what IU soccer stood for, and I had a big brother who provided a very powerful example of leadership. Those perceptions made a strong impression. I started wondering in the distant reaches of my mind what it would be like to play at Indiana University.

But, I dismissed it outright. I was 5 feet, 4 inches tall and thin, nowhere near strong enough, fast enough, big enough, or just plain skilled enough to play there. Besides, I was heading to Michigan State, would reunite with some of my friends in Michigan, and would proudly be my brother Pete's legacy.

Over time, though, that little thought persisted. I can remember walking through a shopping mall one afternoon and seeing an empty lounge with a TV showing a repeat of IU's championship match, a thrilling game in which the Hoosiers beat Duke 1-0 in eight overtimes. That's right, eight overtimes.

Looking back, I find it so strange now, given the wild journey that ensued over the next few years, that a video of this game was replaying then and there, and that I happened upon it.

I sat there, and before I knew it, was mesmerized in a slightly bizarre way. It still kind of creeps me out to think about, but while watching the game, I actually could see myself on the field, playing for IU, like I'd been edited into the video by some modern technological graphics software. Afterward, I thought why not apply to IU, just for snicks and grins? The vision of me playing there grew stronger. I loved the cream and crimson school colors and the beautiful campus; I was inspired by the team-focused, disciplined style of the Hoosiers.

It became so powerful that I actually called Coach Yeagley and set up a meeting, which wasn't much of a meeting, in Bloomington. I drove down with my mom one summer morning, and Coach Yeagley met me in the lobby of the Assembly Hall where his office was located. I had this fantasy that he'd be thrilled to have me play there, maybe even offer me a scholarship. He put that dream to rest pretty quickly while we stood there in the lobby for about 10 minutes.

Indiana had won a national championship, Coach Yeagley gently reminded me, and the team had seven starters coming back from that team. Also, that championship had helped draw some of the best high school seniors in the country to play at Indiana University. Those factors made Coach Yeagley fairly confident that the team had a realistic shot at winning two consecutive national championships.

He was straight with me during those 10 minutes, and I believe that was the kindest thing he could do. There simply was no room for a pretty decent high school player from a modest soccer state like Indiana on the college team that was the best in the nation, he told me. He did say, however, at the very end of the conversation, that if I really wanted to try to play at IU, he would allow me to come to an open tryout a couple weeks into the first semester of school. He could not guarantee, or give me any sense of hope, that I could make the team, but he would let me give it a shot. I believe it was simply a nice gesture on his part, but perhaps it meant a little more than that to me. In the end, I was crushed in some ways but reassured that my intent to go to MSU was a great fit for me.

Until the next morning when I woke up and still felt the strong pull to play at IU, something that I can't really explain all that well—just a force that wouldn't let go.

It was crazy, and a little while later when I shared it with my mom—I could tell my mom anything—she told me I was nuts. But, bless her heart, she said to give it some time. It was our little secret for a couple months. While I trained, I think that anxiety pushed me a little harder. If I was going to try out at Indiana, I'd have to be stronger physically and mentally than I could ever imagine.

But, it really wasn't going to happen. It was the foolish fantasy of an immature kid.

Then, on August 12, 1983—I'll always remember the date because it was the night before my dad and I were going to leave very early in the morning for East Lansing, Michigan, and MSU—I turned everything upside down.

My parents, Deanne, Dino, and I were eating a delicious meal that my mom had prepared as sort of a going away treat, but I wasn't consuming much of it.

My dad was buttoning up the final details: Had I finished packing? Would I be ready to go at 8 the next morning? We were going to meet the coach in the afternoon.

I stared down at my plate, then finally looked up at my dad.

"I've been thinking, Dad," I said.

"Yeah, what is it?"

I couldn't believe what I was about to say. It was crazy. I couldn't get the words out of my mouth.

"Whitey," my dad said. "What is it, son?"

"I want to go to IU," I said, barely above a whisper. "I want to try and play there."

I remember a long silence and then my dad asking me to clarify what the heck I was really trying to tell him. He wanted to know when I'd started thinking about this huge change, when I made the decision. I couldn't bring myself to tell him. Everything was spinning around in my mind. I didn't know how to explain it.

My mom and dad stared at each other; then my dad turned back to me with an expression I'll just call shock.

"I want to play soccer at IU," I said.

He was reeling, trying to remain calm and process what he'd just heard, as was my mom. She didn't know I'd actually decided to act on this delusion. The two of them looked a little dizzy. My dad repositioned himself on the chair a bit. He took a deep breath and let the air out slowly.

"Are you sure?" he finally said in a soft voice. "I mean, have you been thinking about it?"

"Dad," I said, almost chuckling. "It's about all I've been thinking about for the last four months, night and day."

Over the next two hours, we talked, and I basically tried to explain that this little what-if question kept hanging in my mind. What if I am actually good enough to play at IU? Would I wonder for the rest of my life whether I would have made the team? What if I trained my behind off and was able to play for the greatest college soccer program in the nation? What if that question never went away, and I knew it wouldn't now? What if I was sitting in some job at the age of 40, anxious and aggravated with my life, all for squandering this one chance to pursue a wild dream when I was young?

"I'd rather fail at IU," I told my mom and dad, "then spend the rest of my life wondering whether I could have made it."

They had a lot of questions that took a long time to answer. They pointed out that classes were going to start in a few days, and I hadn't registered for any, and that I didn't have housing at IU. I told them we could take care of that in pretty short order—at least, I hoped we could.

Slowly, they came around. I think they saw that I had tried to dismantle this dream with logic and simply couldn't, that it must be a really powerful, enduring force inside me.

I wonder now, as a father and parent, what I would have done in their shoes, and I think the way they handled it was remarkable. They listened, but tested me strongly. In the end, they just didn't want to snuff out this dream.

In that two hours, they gave me an invaluable lesson in leadership as parents. They probably thought I was nuts, but they knew the value of allowing someone to chase a dream—the lessons one can learn, succeed or fail—and they felt very strongly about letting me learn those lessons.

They gave me another leadership lesson right away: taking responsibility for my decisions. They told me that I was the one who was going to call MSU Coach Joe Baum and break the news, which I did at 8 the next morning. He was very professional, saying that I had a spot when I failed at IU, not if but when. Immediately after I hung up the phone, I felt that I'd made a mistake, that I'd gone back on my word, that I had no idea what I was getting myself into.

It was too late. I had to scramble now and live with the chaotic decision I'd just made.

My next call was to Coach Yeagley, who seemed almost as stunned as Coach Baum, and certainly perplexed. After a few seconds, he handed the phone to an assistant who laid out the tryout process and mailed materials to me. About four days later, papers in hand, I packed up the family van and, with my mom, headed south to Bloomington instead of north to East Lansing.

Registering for classes went pretty well. Finding a place to live was a little more of an adventure. I eventually ended up assigned to a lounge at Reed Residence Hall. When we got there, I turned to my mom and said I changed my mind. Too late, she said. Give it a few days, and it'll work out.

Living in a lounge felt like living in the lobby of a chain motel or like I was part of some weird public art exhibit. People would pass through at all times of the day and night. I hated it, and I must have looked pretty pathetic because a few days later, my brother Danny, who had been in Bloomington for pre-season practices, offered me the floor of the apartment he shared with two other soccer players. I took it, and it turned out to be a stroke of great fortune.

His apartment complex, Dunn Hill, was where a lot of soccer players lived, including Pat McGauley, an All-American player at IU who I'd met at a soccer clinic about three years earlier. One day at Dunn Hill we bumped into each other at the mailbox and got to talking. He asked where I was living, and I told him on the dining room floor of my brother's apartment.

I don't know if he felt sorry for me or what. More likely, he was being Pat—a really thoughtful guy. He mentioned that a couple players at Dunn Hill were looking for a roommate after theirs changed his mind about coming back to IU for his junior season. A few minutes later, Pat took me up to their apartment, and a few minutes after that, I had a place to live that wasn't a dining room floor. I also had a couple of extraordinary roommates.

Their names were John Stollmeyer and Keith Meyer. Like Pat, they were All-Americans at IU, two guys who I'd seen play at a sports festival in Indianapolis the summer before. What I remember about watching them was that they drew my entire focus. I kept thinking how much I wanted to play like them.

When we met in their apartment, I could tell pretty quickly that they had distinct personalities. Keith was tall and lean, really handsome, understated, meticulous, well groomed, and all business. "Stolly" was about as opposite in physical and personality makeup as he could be. Maybe two inches shorter than Keith, Stolly was all thick muscle as if carved from granite, scruffy, a dreamer with an energetic, outgoing personality that some perceived as a little rough around the edges, even abrasive. But he had a really big heart, as I would find out soon. And, he loved to laugh.

The two of them were somewhat of an odd couple but really close friends. In fact, Keith had persuaded Stolly to come to IU. They were starters next to each other on the field and would remain starters, roommates, and close friends for the next three years.

I moved in, and things went pretty well. Both guys were friendly, and I was conscious of not overstepping my place. Stolly, who I shared a room with, took me grocery shopping and showed me how to do laundry. They had distinctly different views on my plan to try out for the soccer team. Stolly's take was why not go for it? I had nothing to lose. Keith was a little more skeptical and thought I might be wasting my time. I appreciated both perspectives.

The team had been practicing for a couple weeks by the time I arrived. Tryouts wouldn't be held for a couple more weeks. During that time, I'd walk to a church parking lot where I could see practices through a fence and get an idea of just how strong a national championship team was. The answer is very, very strong, and I started having doubts again, thinking about how everybody back home except my family thought I had no chance of making it.

After watching for a few minutes, I'd go for long runs and then train on my own, gaining extra fuel from my anxiety of watching the 34 guys on IU's team work out.

On the first day of tryouts, I was an emotional wreck. I hadn't slept the night before, and all I could think about until tryouts started at 3:30 p.m. was whether I'd made the right decision. When the time came and I stood on the soccer field surrounded by about 20 other guys, I soon discovered that the range of talent was vast. At least seven were high-caliber players every bit as strong, if not stronger, than I was.

It was hot and muggy, and the tryout was grueling. We'd run three-minute, one-on-one games, rest for three minutes, and then go again. Then assistant coaches, who ran the tryout, progressed to two-on-two and finally three-on-three games. It was the most intense competition I've experienced on the soccer field. Tempers flared, and I was worried that my style of play, which always had focused on team rather than individual success, was going unnoticed. I needed every ounce of training and mental toughness to hang in there. But, I made up my mind about one thing: I was not going to be cut from the IU soccer team for lack of effort.

Finally, at the end of the three-day tryout, came one very extreme half hour of soccer. Coach Yeagley stepped from leading the "real team" on the regular practice field to watch us scruffy mutts on the tryout field. He would help the assistant coaches decide if any of us were worthy to wear the cream and crimson. After watching us beat on each other, Coach Yeagley passed out slips of paper and pencils and asked us to write down the name of one guy, excluding ourselves, we thought should make the team. Then he and the assistants huddled for 15 minutes and returned to the group. Coach Yeagley thanked everyone for their effort and announced they were keeping one guy.

Me.

Chills swept over me, and I felt like I was floating. A couple guys came over and congratulated me, but I was so overwhelmed I'm not sure how, or if, I responded. I was sort of dazed, thrilled beyond explanation, relieved, more exhausted than I'd ever been. I thought about all the people who'd told me I had no chance. I simply could not believe it had happened.

I ran back to the apartment and called my parents. When my mom answered the phone and I told her, I swear she broke into a Greek tribal celebration dance. My dad called me from work and followed that up with a letter—he's a big letter writer—that arrived a couple days later. Stolly and Keith both congratulated me but neither said much. They were pretty focused on winning a second consecutive national championship.

The next day's sunrise was a bright one, which was appropriate. I was about to get a very rude awakening and start on what would be the most challenging journey of my life.

Coaches designated me as a red shirt. For those unfamiliar with the workings of the National Collegiate Athletic Association, red-shirting allows a player to practice with the team, but he or she is prohibited from playing in a game or even sitting on the bench in a game. It's designed to give a player who may need more time to develop an extra year to do so. In my case, I think it might have been a way for the coaches to stick me in a sort of limbo. They liked me well enough and wanted to reward me for hard work, but probably also knew that making me a red shirt would help me see the futility of my expectations and lead me to quit.

It was rough. I was barely the 35th man on a 35-man team. Some days I wouldn't even get a chance to play in practice scrimmages. Coaches barely knew my name. I don't think I ever had to pass out towels or water, but I got really good at moving goals, retrieving soccer balls, and performing other grunt and "go-fer" tasks. It was humiliating.

But it was a great leadership lesson, although I was completely unaware of that at the time. Apart from the lesson that leaders must learn to persevere through adverse circumstances, I learned it was up to me to choose my attitude, to decide how I was going to handle this opportunity. I learned that staying optimistic was a conscious, ongoing effort, and that's what I tried really hard to do. I focused on being proud that I was one of 35 guys on the best team in the country, that maybe 500,000 kids across the country would give their left foot to be part of the IU soccer program.

And, like I did watching my parents while growing up, I got to see what leadership looks like every single day—on the soccer field and in the apartment. As team captains, Stolly and Keith set an extremely high bar for work ethic that spilled over to the apartment. Almost every night, they'd talk soccer. Sometimes it was general thoughts; other times it was specific to an upcoming game. Both of them also took me under their wings. Keith would call me to his room, where he had a rocking chair, and tell me to sit and talk about how things were going. It was his way of keeping tabs on me and keeping me on track, crucial skills for a team leader. Stolly focused more on what I might call my social development, but he'd also take me on long walks late at night through IU's beautiful campus where both of us would share a number of our doubts and vulnerabilities.

Small signs of improvement sprouted about halfway through that season when I was allowed to scrimmage against the starters in practice once in a while. When I had a decent performance, Stolly or Keith would come up to me individually and acknowledge that I'd played well. That was another important leadership lesson: caring for your fellow human beings, the importance of taking a moment or two to show some kindness when you don't have to, when it probably doesn't matter to anyone but that individual who really needs it at that moment. Leaders need to look for chances to say a word or two of encouragement to even the people who play the smallest role in the organization. Those words were a tremendous lift to me, more precious than gold. I believe that a kind word can be what motivates a person to hang in there, and hanging in there can be the difference between success and failure. The kind words and gestures of Stolly, Keith, and others created in me the very powerful intention that I was going to treat others the way those thoughtful people who boosted me up had treated me in those lowly times when I deeply needed it. To this day, that's a central part of who I am.

What Stolly, Keith, Coach Yeagley, and others brought together worked well again that season. Indiana University took a second consecutive national championship, a 1-0 overtime win against Columbia University in Ft. Lauderdale, an extra-exciting run for me because my brother Danny was on the team. The celebration in the team hotel that night was crazy, as you might imagine, and Stolly and Keith erased a lot of the sting of me being a redshirt by going out of their way to make me feel like I was part of the team celebration and that I had contributed all year long—another example of thoughtful leadership that made a powerful impression on me.

It might sound laughable to some people, but being the 35th man on a national championship roster felt like more of an accomplishment than being a starter on a team that wins as many games as it loses. Whatever small piece I was of that national championship team I had earned the hard way: by sweating and grinding through every practice, every day, week in and week out with absolutely no glory or notoriety of any kind. That realization, the relationships I was beginning to develop, and the fantastic season fired up my drive and desire for the next year. I actually started visualizing each and every step of my dream, from making the roster to making the traveling team to becoming a sub off the bench to becoming a starter.

The coaching staff had a decidedly different perspective and, in my evaluation at the end of the season, they made their position pretty clear.

"You're never going to play here, Whitey," Coach Yeagley told me. I started getting this sick feeling in the pit of my stomach. He went on to say some of the same things he told me at our meeting in Assembly Hall months earlier: that the team had a number of returning players and was expecting another all-star class of high school recruits.

"We'd suggest that you transfer to another school, Whitey," Coach Yeagley said, "if in fact you want to continue playing soccer in college."

I was reeling but begged to hang with the team through the more informal, shorter spring season. The coaches agreed but were unmoved during evaluations after that season. They still didn't think I should be on the team. I asked for another chance, and they grudgingly agreed to let me try out again. I wouldn't be allowed to stay in the dorms with the rest of the team when they arrived early in August, they said, and if I wanted to eat with the team, I had to pay my own way.

It wasn't much of a chance, but I took it. Over summer, I played in a tournament for IU assistant coach Mike Freitag on an Indiana State Team and did well enough that he mentioned it to Coach Yeagley. That tournament also was really exciting for me because it was the first time my brothers Pete and Danny and I were on the same team.

Weeks later, I showed up on campus for pre-season training and somehow survived two-a-day practices to actually make the 34-man roster. I was relieved and at least a little hopeful. Being one of the 34 meant I would suit up for every home game, but only 18 to 20 guys were allowed to travel to away games. And, for almost all of those away games, coaches held out two slots for guys based on how well they'd practiced in the days leading up to the game.

Competition for those slots could get pretty vicious among scrubs like me. Some days, fights broke out. I remember having really strong practice weeks and never having my name called. I made the travel team once and that time only because coaches decided to take 25 players. It was pretty depressing, physically and psychologically exhausting.

But I learned another life leadership lesson during that time. I started noticing that at least a few of the guys in my circumstances were angry and pessimistic. Some quit. What I realized was that those guys who stayed around but griped the entire way were sapping my motivation. As part of a subconscious survival mechanism, I drifted away from them and hung around the optimistic guys and the guys who were playing.

What I realized was that by surrounding myself with high-achieving, optimistic, and encouraging guys, I kept that same attitude, which would be crucial if I wanted to achieve my dream. I understand now, decades later, how important that is for people who want to be leaders at any level of an organization: Surround yourselves with can-do, enthusiastic, hardworking people. Shed or avoid the whiners.

Stolly and Keith would offer me a ride to practice just about every day, and I took them up on their offers. They almost always arrived early and stayed late, which meant I did, too. My playing improved, which shouldn't come as a big surprise to anyone who understands that focused, additional work almost always leads to improved performance.

As one of the 34 guys who suited up for every home game, I did get chances to play, but only in the last three minutes when we were leading 5 or 7 or 9 to nothing. It's called garbage time, and when my name was called, I'd cringe but pop off the bench and go in for my 90 seconds of glory. The funny thing is that, even though fans were sort of laughing at me and other guys who played mop-up-minutes, after a few seconds, my mind would let go of all the embarrassment and embrace my love of the game. All I saw was me playing soccer for Indiana University, the best darn college soccer team in the country. That made me feel pretty appreciative, believe it or not.

Then came the Ohio State game.

A little past the middle of the season, the team was taking a bus to Columbus, Ohio, to play the Buckeyes. Coaches said anybody who found their own way to the game would suit up and have a shot at playing. I was pretty reluctant. Short on cash, I thought if the coaches really wanted me to go, they would have found room on the bus.

Stolly disagreed and talked me through it, mostly by saying I should suck up my pride and demonstrate to the coaches and players how committed I was to being part of the team. I stewed about it for a couple of days and then borrowed a car, scraped together gas money, packed a few sandwiches and drinks, and followed the team bus like some weird groupie. I was the only guy who drove, but actually had a pretty fun time waving and joking around with the guys while we rolled down the highway together.

Just as the coaches promised, I suited up. We won, and I didn't play a single second.

After the game, feeling like an ignoramus, I waited for the bus to leave the parking lot, hung back awhile longer, then hit the road for the long drive back alone—a 230-mile trip filled with a lot of anger, self-pity, embarrassment, and soul searching. By the time I'd arrived at the apartment, long after the team had returned to Bloomington, I felt that I'd mostly made peace with the decision. But just beneath the surface, I was still pretty upset.

I trudged up the steps, came through the door, and there was Stolly, studying at the kitchen table. He knew I'd be looking for him, and he wanted to be there for me. I guess all the hurt rushed over and through me, nearly two years of it. I broke down sobbing. He got up and gave me a hug, sat me down, and told me that he still felt I did the right thing.

He let me continue crying and venting and griping but stopped me when I started running down the coaches. That was another leadership lesson he taught me: Don't direct responsibility elsewhere when it should be on your shoulders. Besides, bitching about a coach leads a player to pout, and pouting often can lead to an exit from the team. Stolly knew I wanted to be on that team, wanted it very badly. He wanted me on the team almost as badly, too, and later would demonstrate just how strongly he felt.

The one bright spot during all this darkness wore crutches and got out of a car across the street from my apartment one cloudy fall day. I would later discover that her name was Sherri Seger, but all I knew that day was that something about her drew me to her. She was beautiful, to be sure, but she also had something I couldn't really articulate. A style, a grace, a warmth. I sensed all that almost from the moment I saw her and wanted to rush down there and help her across the street, but I was very intimidated. I simply watched for those few seconds.

It turns out that Sherri had come to IU on a gymnastics scholarship but had injured her ankle badly, undergone one surgery, and then a second after the first one was unsuccessful. It also turned out that she lived in the same apartment complex as I did and that she and her roommates were friends with one of my soccer buddies, Mickey McCartney, and his roommates. Small world.

I developed a full-fledged secret crush on Sherri, although I knew that I had no chance with her. Mickey was the only person who was aware, and he kept it confidential but would ask me about it once in a while. In the end, I admired Sherri, wanted to get to know her, and thought it would be great to count her among my friends. But, even though she lived beneath Mickey's apartment, I didn't run into her for weeks until I was walking through the training room at Assembly Hall and she was working on some therapy on her ankle.

I thought this might be my chance to make my Big Move, but I panicked. I was only able to say hi and then kept right on walking, not knowing what else to say. As pathetic as that move had been, I now knew where I could find Sherri. So, over the next few weeks, I would make almost daily runs through the training room to pick up ice or check in with the trainer to see if there were any new developments in the field of athletic training that I needed to know.

Time went by, and we did get to know each other a little as part of a group of about 15 friends who hung out together. I was glad to discover that she was exactly who I thought she was—a gentle, kind, happy woman with a big, electric smile that she displayed often. But, I still knew I didn't have a chance.

On the soccer field, my exploits continued to be pretty futile. I was working my rear end off and getting next to no game time. Meanwhile, this year's version of the Hoosiers soccer team was looking like it would contend for a third consecutive national championship. We were rugged, smart, and very team-oriented. As captains, Stolly and Keith kept up their relentless pursuit of excellence, continuing to arrive early and stay late. All the guys had a burning commitment to be great, independent from any pushing from coaches. I later learned that was another important leadership lesson—find a way to motivate your team members to take an internal, personal responsibility for being great, and for holding themselves accountable. If you've got that going on, chances are you've got one very effective juggernaut.

And, that's what we were that year. We won our first eight games before playing a tie, then followed that with a 10-game winning streak. We ended the regular season with 19 wins, 1 loss, and 1 tie and were primed to go for a three-peat.

Although I didn't make the post-season roster—another really debilitating blow—the guys tore through the tournament and got to the championship where they faced Clemson in Seattle in late November.

But a third consecutive championship eluded us. The game went late, tied at 1-1. Then the Tigers scored and beat us 2-1. To say the guys were devastated would be a huge understatement. As hard as it was to acknowledge then, time passed, and I understood what a fantastic season it was, a season that every team in the country but Clemson would have died to experience.

For Keith, that final game placed him in pretty rare company. He was one of two IU players in the history of the program to play in the NCAA Championship final game in each of his years on the team. Says a lot about the caliber of the teams we had and Keith's leadership skills and winning mentality. After graduation, he played professionally in Kansas City, married his longtime girlfriend, and raised a family. His son Tommy fell in love with soccer, too, and ended up playing at IU and wearing number 20 on his jersey, same as his father wore a couple of decades earlier.

The one saving grace in those dismal winter days was that I knew Stolly, who had another year before graduation, would be there when we returned. That gave me a little spark to carry on.

Evaluations, always a time of high anxiety for me, loomed. I figured this year my chances of moving way up on the roster were pretty strong. I'd gotten a little playing time in the regular season, and I'd kept my upbeat, team-healthy energy going throughout. We also were losing seven starters.

About a week after the Clemson game, I sat in Coach Yeagley's office with him and a couple other coaches. The meeting was short—maybe four minutes—and not very sweet. They essentially told me they had no idea where I fit and that they'd learn a lot after spring season. It was less than reassuring. In fact, the tone of Coach Yeagley's voice made me very nervous.

I played well that spring in limited chances but that failed to impress Coach Yeagley. At my evaluation, he told me again that I was never going to play at IU; that I just didn't have the level of talent needed; that I should transfer to a less-competitive program. I knew why he said that. We were expecting what was thought to be the most talented group of freshman soccer players in the country. The coaches had no room for some mutt walk-on like me. It was almost as if, with each year of experience I gained, I also was being squeezed out by this never-ending stream of young superstars coming to IU. I was in no-man's land without a lifeline.

I was overwhelmed with hurt and fear for my future. One thing became clear: I needed to look elsewhere.

That opportunity actually had surfaced a few weeks earlier. When the team played the championship in Seattle, I couldn't make the trip. My family hosted a party to watch the game, and one of my high school teammates, Ken Veilands, showed up. We chatted about his experience playing at University of Southern Indiana, a competitive team that competed in a lower level of the NCAA known as Division II. He sang the praises of the program and the school and told me I could play there right now. I was intrigued and told him to go ahead and pass my name to USI coach, Mike Ferrell.

A few days later, Coach Ferrell called, and we talked over burgers at a restaurant in Carmel. He gave me an even stronger pitch than Ken, and by the time we finished, I was giving serious thought to becoming a USI Screaming Eagle.

That lasted for exactly one sleepless night.

I just couldn't leave Indiana University. My dream of playing there would not fade. I knew deep inside me that I wanted to push myself to the very limit and then some to play for the best team in the nation, and I guess I thought a sliver of hope still existed. I got back to Coach Ferrell the next day, and he understood completely. That spring I played just well enough to get invited to pre-season training with the team in August. I was entering my third year, and my existence was as precarious as ever. Then a reason for renewed hope emerged. I called it the Stolly Initiative.

Being from Virginia, Stolly was unable to get home a lot during his time at Indiana. So, I regularly invited him to my parents' place. They loved him, and we became even closer.

Throughout our time at IU, he was bummed that we'd never gotten on the field together in a game. That summer, he decided to try and make it happen. He was staying in Bloomington for summer school and offered to train with me.

"I'm going to teach you the toughness you need, and, come fall, you'll be ready," he told me, "readier than you've ever been. When the season starts, you and I are going to be on that field together, Whitey. Me at center mid; you at left mid. And, we're gonna kick some ass."

I couldn't turn down that offer. Stolly was one of the most rugged, tenacious players in the nation. Any lessons he was willing to impart I was willing to work at and absorb.

Alternating between my parents' house and Bloomington, we trained almost every day in the hot, humid summer of central and south central Indiana, often three times a day. We'd run distances and sprints over and over. We competed head-to-head in drills. It was beyond grueling.

Throughout every drill, Stolly made it clear he was not there to make me feel good about myself. He was there to make me work harder, and he did that by beating me time and time again, every day, then telling me specifically what I needed to do with each drill. It was tough love from a guy who knew all about tenacity. This summer training program was the ideal platform for him to show it. He pushed me past my breaking point, making me understand that the only way he was going to make me feel good about myself was if I outworked him.

Progress was slow, but by early August, I could last as long as he could most times. My game started to get stronger and more precise. My confidence grew. By the time we reported early to pre-season training, I was a machine, tougher than I'd ever been mentally and physically.

Those few weeks taught me another important lesson for leadership and for life in general. Hard work—really hard, focused work—is a skill, just like agility or speed or jumping ability or hand-eye and foot-eye coordination. It's a little different in that hard work is a skill you develop. Too often, I think, we place all this emphasis on natural talent, or smarts. Those can play a part. But the more I go through life, the more I appreciate that choosing the right attitude, getting back up after being knocked down, staying motivated and focused on hard work, and being resourceful are what matter in life.

All that effort from Stolly and me coalesced at the perfect time. He and I and a few others reported to pre-season practices a few days early, a tradition for IU soccer upperclassmen. We'd play in these 6-on-6 scrimmages, and they got pretty tough because everybody knew a lot of positions were going to be open this season. I jumped into the fray and played well, better than I'd played in practices. I had that edge I'd been missing. Guys noticed and mentioned it to me, specifically Stolly, and Stolly didn't BS people. He told me I was going to be something special this year, that I was going to make a difference. I felt the same way.

It was the last night of scrimmages before the formal pre-season practices began, and I was playing without fatigue or pain all the way through the final scrimmage in the wonderful hot, thick night of August in Bloomington, Indiana. Toward the end of the scrimmage, the ball came toward me, and I got to it, planted my right foot, took a shot with my left, and felt something pop in that foot I'd planted. Didn't think anything of it, really. I'd heard plenty of snaps and pops from my body over the years. I kept playing for another 15 minutes or so, feeling the pain hanging on but at the same time feeling that if I was able to crack it—sort of like cracking a knuckle or a finger to pop it back in place—I would be fine.

Except that I wasn't able to crack it back in place, and the pain kept hanging on. After practice, I got some ice, and Stolly hauled me back to the apartment where I placed the bag on my foot. I tried to step on it a couple of times and pain throbbed along the outside of my right foot.

"Stolly," I told him, "I think this is more than what I thought it was."

I was right.

After a trip to the emergency room that night and two visits with our team athletic trainer, Johnny Schrader, over the next two days, I got a definitive diagnosis: I'd fractured the fifth metatarsal on my right foot. I didn't even know there was a bone called a metatarsal.

Johnny explained it's a long bone that extends behind the baby toe, and that I had endured a Jones fracture (named for the British doctor who researched and wrote about the injury), a break in that metatarsal that typically is one of the slowest healing bones in the body. The reason is that blood circulation—critical to bone healing—is very minimal in that spot. Even after someone recovers from a Jones fracture, it often reoccurs.

For me, it meant the season was over before it began. I was going to need to wear a non-weight-bearing cast for 10 to 12 weeks, Johnny said. It also meant I might need surgery if it didn't recover properly, another common occurrence with Jones fractures. The worst case scenario? Some Jones fractures are so chronic that they end an athlete's career.

I had no emotion for this. It was staggering. It felt like a trap door had been pulled from under me, and I was falling into a black, empty void. In about 36 hours, I went from being poised to seize the dream I'd worked so hard for, playing for the best college soccer team in the nation, to being shut down for the entire season—maybe for the rest of my life. I just stared at Johnny for I don't know how long.

"I'm sorry, Whitey," he said. "Let's not get too far ahead of ourselves. Let's take a look at it again after 10 to 12 weeks and see what we've got; see how well it's doing."

He put a cast on right there, and I kept the crutches I'd gotten a couple of nights earlier. Stolly took me home and then headed to practice. I knew coaches would barely shrug at the loss of a guy like me. In the apartment alone, I started what would be a very steep downward spiral. I thought about how hard I'd worked and how little time I'd have left to achieve the dream, if I even had another chance. I thought about being unable to play with Stolly. It was the lowest I'd ever been, and I didn't see a way out. I was looking for pity, which I got for a while, and I knew one thing for sure: I was ready to quit this asinine dream.

But, at some point, stewing in my own self-pity, I started to get a little angry—at myself. I started struggling back and forth between the part of me that that wanted to feel sorry and point blame everywhere I looked, including in the mirror, and with the persistent optimist who is at my core. After a few days, I got sick of the whiny crybaby. That simply is not who I am, thank God. I tossed the crybaby to the side to make room for the real me.

From that moment, I started thinking I hadn't really gone the full distance and that I didn't want to be the person that killed my dream. I thought about how much I loved the game at this place at this time, my love of a challenge, and my love of the journey, no matter how treacherous and arduous it can get. In a strange way, the idea of staying, hanging in there and working through this ordeal, taking ownership, was empowering. And, that was a lot more fun and exciting than feeling sorry for myself.

So, I planned how I would return. It came down to attending every practice on time and staying in shape. Over the next 10 weeks, I made each practice, and the guys got to see my pretty innovative, entertaining workouts. I'd hop on a stationary bicycle in the training room and ride it with my one good leg for an hour. Then I'd go up to the cinder block track around the field at Armstrong Stadium and hobble-jump on my crutches around the track for two miles. It was tough, particularly battling the negativity and lethargy that crept into my mind from time to time. But I'd drag myself through the routine, and every time I did, I felt a little hope, like I was moving forward, even if only baby steps on crutches.

I also attended every game, serving as something of a bench jockey cheerleader. I made a conscious decision to be grateful to remain a part of the team. Was it difficult and awkward at times? You bet. But here's another little secret about pursuing your dreams: You can't care too much about how silly you may look. You just have to get after it.

In mid-October, I got the cast removed, but whether I'd fully healed was still an uncertainty. I had to go through weeks of rehab, starting with walking without a limp on concrete, then moving to grass and doing the same. After I was limp-free walking on those surfaces, I then was to run on concrete, then grass without a limp—and without pain.

Guess what? The persistent optimist won. By mid-November, Johnny cleared me to participate in one, 15-minute drill at a practice. I never enjoyed a drill so much. I think I smiled the entire time and looked forward to the next day when we would face University of Evansville in the second round of the post-season tournament.

We lost. Our season was done. My third year amounted to one practice drill.

At the perpetually anxious evaluations, coaches gave me little reason for hope, telling me they had no idea where I fit. Can't say I was shocked. Hey, at least they remembered my name.

Stolly ended up being drafted by the Cleveland Force professional indoor team, where he played for a couple of years. He also played for the US national team in the 1987 Pan American Games, then for the US in the 1988 Olympics and 1990 World Cup. Like me, he settled in the Indianapolis area, and we in fact did end up playing together in an over-40 league. We still see each other regularly.

Although that third year was a lost one for me in many ways, I did learn the invaluable leadership lessons of persistence, patience, and choosing your attitude. I also started what would be another powerful, lifelong friendship that became strong and enduring, oddly enough, because of devastating, unimaginable loss.

Pete Stoyanovich was a three-sport athlete out of Dearborn, Michigan, who I met when he visited Indiana on a recruiting trip. He committed and was so coveted that coaches at IU allowed him to play football and soccer, an almost unheard of setup back then. It created a whirlwind schedule for him, where he would zip around on a golf cart to participate in both practices during a typical day. On weekends, he'd hop on buses and planes to play for the football and soccer teams. Pete's existence was so rare that *Sports Illustrated* visited the campus for a feature about him. It would be an early example of Pete's celebrity and athletic prowess.

But he also was overwhelmed his freshman year, the same year I was injured and rehabbing my physical and psychological wounds. By his sophomore year, Pete had adapted much better. My future started looking a little brighter, too. I had a pretty decent spring season, stayed in pretty strong shape over the summer, worked really hard in pre-season practices, and ended up being one of the first subs off the bench once the season started.

Seven games into the season, one of our starters got injured and was done for the season. In the locker room minutes before the next contest, a home game against St. Louis University, Coach Yeagley called the team together to announce the starting lineup, which included one very significant surprise name: mine.

I felt goosebumps sweep over me. A couple guys, including Pete, who also was a starter, slapped me on the back. A few others actually clapped. I heard a whoop or two. Four seasons into an impossible journey, I'd started my first game at Indiana University. I'd somehow managed to pull myself to the top.

But I quickly tumbled down.

I was just too nervous, and I let the nerves overtake me. Instead of playing the fired-up style that had gotten me there, I played tentatively, thinking that I didn't want to blow this chance. That turned out to be another valuable leadership teaching moment: Remember what got you to the top, to the professional excellence that you've achieved; trust and stay with those core skills and values.

We lost 3-1 in an embarrassing game that was something of a microcosm of our season. After last year's disappointing season—we'd won 12, lost 8, and made an early exit from the post-season tournament— leadership on this year's team had gotten off track. Much as I loved the guys, individual objectives had replaced team goals.

Coaches certainly picked up on the dynamic and were so angry they told us to take the next day off and clear our heads. But then, they called a team meeting, which another teammate and I missed because word hadn't gotten to us on the golf course (no cell phones back then) where we'd gone to clear our heads.

At the meeting, Coach Yeagley noted that the major problem with the loss was me; that I'd been responsible for two of St. Louis' goals. When I'd heard what occurred in the meeting, I was hurt and angry and arranged a meeting with Coach Yeagley. We sat in his office with two assistants, and I apologized for missing the meeting. Then he played game film of the two goals, saying I should have gotten to the ball before the St. Louis players did in both cases where they went on to score. I disagreed, but it didn't matter. I fell silent while I listened to them pick me apart for a few more moments.

After that, I rode the bench game after game, never even getting a glance from Coach Yeagley. Team atmosphere was deteriorating, too. We were dividing into factions. Discipline was unraveling. We were goofing off on the bench. And we kept losing games we should have won.

Throughout all that, one of the things that kept me going was my casual friendship with Pete Stoyanovich, who came to be called Stoyo. He was a really fun, down-to-earth guy who loved to laugh. We had similar ethnic backgrounds—his Macedonian, mine Greek. Family was important to him, as was working hard, just like it's important to me. On the rare times I'd see him other than in practice or games, we always sought each other out and had a few laughs.

He was a handsome, charismatic guy who looked like he had the world by the tail, but his hectic schedule left him a little untethered without any really close friends on campus. I actually think he might have been kind of lonely. And, so, when his world exploded in October of 1986, I'm sure he felt very much alone, angry, and confused, but mostly overwhelmed with grief.

He had tragically and abruptly lost his mother, the person he was closest with throughout his life.

It's a curious thing about human nature. When real heartbreak happens to a person, the instinct for many is avoidance. We feel awkward, even helpless; we don't want to upset the grieving person more. I'm wired a little differently. When I heard about the death of Stoyo's mother, I, too, didn't know how to respond. But I knew this much: The guy needed somebody, and I decided that the very least I could do was be there when he returned to his dorm. Just be present for him.

So, I waited outside his room on a Sunday night, and when he showed up, he was alone. He wasn't perplexed by the sight of me. Wasn't uncomfortable. Wasn't angry. He unlocked the door to his room, set down his luggage, embraced me, and started sobbing, and so did I.

I'm not sure what I said or if I said anything at all. What transpired in that room was a blur. It was overwhelming and really painful, but it demonstrated something life affirming, too: the value of presence. That was an epiphany for me.

Sometimes all we need is each other. If we have that authentic presence, we have something more resilient than loss, something that enables us to carry on.

From that moment on, Stoyo and I shared a close, almost indescribable bond. We hung out together all the time. I brought him home for weekends when his schedule permitted, and my family embraced him, which was really easy to do.

While that relationship strengthened and deepened, my soccer prospects continued on a flat, hopeless track. Game after game after game—I think I lost track at 8 or 10—I rode the bench. It gave me the chance to do a little soul-searching, and I kept coming back to my experience with Stoyo. It provided great perspective. It helped me stop worrying about my own troubles and take a larger view to understand that soccer is just a game, a game that can teach valuable lessons about how leaders build a team and about life, but still a game. I started to relax, even surrendered in a way.

Our team was languishing, goofing around on the bench way too much. On the field, players were losing focus, pointing fingers, and giving up. I was as guilty as anybody, and after a while, it started to make me sick to my stomach. The whole situation came to a head after a loss to Clemson. Several of us went out after the game and got caught missing curfew. Now, we were saying to heck with the rules. We were making our own rules.

The coaches had seen enough and gave us a stern talk at a team meeting before our next game, which was against American University. They warned of suspensions, pretty serious stuff. But, when I looked around the room, I saw some guys mocking one of the coaches who spoke. Well, that session woke me up. I'd made up my mind then and there. I might not be able to rally all the guys, but I could at least set an example, even from the bench. I was done being lackadaisical. I'd seize every opportunity that came my way to support the broader team goals, and I'd be enthusiastic about it. That was what guys like Stolly, Keith, Pat McGauley, and a handful of others had taught me, and it seemed to work pretty well then.

I didn't have to wait too long to seize the moment.

Against American, a team we typically would dispose of without too much effort, I watched from the bench while we played anemic soccer and were down 1-0 at the half. My aggravation had peaked. Coaches were at a loss for words when we gathered in a loose circle under a shady tree near the field. So I decided to jump in and say what needed to be said. I stood and made my way to the center of the circle. I could see guys staring at me, wondering what the heck I was doing.

"Look," I said, "I know I sit on the bench. I've sat on the bench for four years, and I'm okay with that. But here's the situation: It's one thing to sit on the bench and watch a team play hard, play for each other, and not reach expectations. But, sitting on the bench watching you guys play is (bleeping) pathetic. It's embarrassing. It's insulting. That I will not stand for. Who in the (bleep) do you think you're playing for? When are we going to get our heads out of our asses and start playing like a (bleeping) team, guys, like a team IU can be proud of?"

Those are the highlights of what was about a two-minute, purple rant. I rarely cuss, and I'd never done anything like that in my life. Everyone, including the coaches, was completely silent. They probably thought I was nuts, but that's okay.

It worked for at least a little. We rallied and finished with a tie. I didn't play a minute, but I did play in the next game at the University of Evansville, a really raucous place that I love. With something like 15 minutes left and us down 1-0, Coach Yeagley called my name, and I gave the team all the enthusiasm and energy I could. Late in the game, one of their players tripped me deliberately—probably in response to an unintentional, but physical, exchange I'd had with their goalie a couple of minutes earlier. Refs gave us a penalty kick, and our guy Chris Keenan scored, which allowed us to eke out a 1-1 tie in overtime.

The season was winding down, and we needed a strong finish merely to make the post-season tournament. Not getting there was unheard of at IU. That had happened only twice in the 32-year history of the men's program.

After our quasi-rally at Evansville, we were pretty jacked, and practices that week were crisp and focused. But we couldn't transfer it to the games. We lost our last two, and the season ended with us being left out of the post-season tournament. We also were the first team in IU history to fall short of 10 wins.

A certain downward spiral was building, and it carried over to the off-season when some guys were caught drinking and carousing. Coach Yeagley took a tough stance. By the time everything got sorted out, six of our best, most highly recruited athletes were done playing at IU—some kicked off the team, some transferred, and some graduated. It was almost as if somebody had driven a truck through the center of the team photo. We'd gotten pretty low, but the truth is, I was unsure if we'd hit rock bottom yet. Coach Yeagley was reeling and later would tell me this was perhaps the lowest point in a coaching career that spanned four decades.

And, yet deep inside, the persistent optimist in me looked at the scraps that remained and felt a little spark. Indiana soccer still was Indiana soccer, with guys who'd gotten there by performing at a pretty high level. Maybe this moment was created for a reason, I thought. Maybe now, finally, was my chance to take everything that had stood in my way on this journey and use it to build a personal dream that, in the end, could be a leadership code.

Stoyo and I talked about it a lot in the months before pre-season training. We both still had our doubts—he more than I. To this day, I remember one recent alum of the program saying we'd be lucky to win five games.

I thought it was possible that the housecleaning had left a group that was unsteady and a little fragmented but also had the talent to at least compete. We'd bottomed out, I thought, and it felt to me that the team might be starting to climb out of the hole.

Stoyo's situation gave me enormously valuable perspective, and I'd gotten a boost at the end of last season by receiving the team's Mental Attitude Award. In the spring season, I went back to my grinder status, looking to bring high energy and making it contagious by being pretty vocal, upbeat, and encouraging with the guys. Then, while home over the summer, Coach Yeagley called with a surprise: a scholarship for my final year. Until then, I was paying the full freight of going to school. His offer was so exciting that I just kept thanking him.

My life off the field also perked up considerably. The reason was Sherri Seger, that beautiful young lady I'd seen hobble across the street about a year earlier. I was seeing a lot more of her now. In fact, we were a couple thanks to a night right after finals when a group of us went out dancing, and Sherri and I finally had a chance to talk. Our long conversation flowed into dawn, and our relationship began the next day.

It was better than I dreamed it could be. As a college athlete, Sherri understood all that I was experiencing and striving for, and she helped. Most important of all was her Catholic faith, which was a central force in her life. While I'd been raised in a spiritual household, I'd fallen away in my late teens and early 20s. When we started dating, Sherri and I made mass a regular part of our weekend, and it reopened a door to me. For decades now, my faith in God, my regular attendance in church, and my daily ritual of prayer and other involvement in my church is as vital to me as the blood that runs through my veins.

The result of all this was that I was emotionally centered, committed, enthusiastic, and in great shape. Plus, I had the lessons of more than four years at IU—and my upbringing before that—to guide me. I knew that team chemistry and camaraderie can take a group a long way, even if overall star power is a little dim, and I thought we had a chance, however slim, of making a run if we could start liking each other again and get back to playing aggressive, high energy, self-sacrificing soccer for each other. If we could embrace accountability and have fun working our asses off, we might be pretty tough.

Then, something truly special happened.

At our first team meeting the night before we were to start two-a-day, pre-season practices, Coach Yeagley shook things up by saying he would pick captains, choices the team typically makes by voting at the end of the pre-season. He selected goalie Bruce Killough, a former high school All-American and member of the US National Team who was all business, hardworking, and had a team-first attitude. An excellent choice.

And then Coach Yeagley pointed in my direction. I felt something in my chest jump.

"And, Whitey," he said. "Whitey Kapsalis."

I was stunned speechless, overwhelmed. I could see Coach Yeagley's mouth move, and I heard the words "doing things right," "integrity," "character," "role model," and others. But my head was spinning so fast and pounding so hard, I wasn't processing all of it. Me, the kid who would never play at IU, the kid who was told to transfer, the kid who lost an entire season—and almost a career—to injury, was team captain.

I ran back to my apartment, called my parents and Sherri, and they were thrilled beyond words. When I hung up the phone, I couldn't help but sit there a few moments and shake my head at what an unpredictable, fascinating journey life can be. What places we can go if we just open ourselves to the possible, get after it with everything we can give, and keep in mind that achievement is always best when shared.

Now it was time to get to work. Next morning at the first day's practice, I set a personal best of 11 minutes and 34 seconds in the notorious two-mile run that marks the opening of two-a-days. I finished third among our team, and I think I set the agenda that we were going to push ourselves harder than ever—that for us to succeed, we had to be tougher than everybody else.

As the days passed, I was looking for different ways to pull the team together and make the ride a fun one. I hit on music, which can be such a powerful unifying force. The song, "Back in the High Life Again," by Steve Winwood clicked in my head. It's a song that was popular at the time with a chorus that includes the phrase, "all the doors I closed one time will open up again." Its relevance was pretty obvious. Seemed like the perfect theme for us, in fact. I started playing it in the locker room, and it soon became a regular selection before games.

I wanted to be sure we were building that team bond in another way by being a little goofy, which takes a little pressure off. One of my favorite go-to moves came when I'd lead stretches, which I did almost every day. The problem was that I had zero flexibility. So, I came up with a few "stretches" that made me and the rest of the team look ridiculous, such as the Whitey Stretch. In that exercise, we'd bend at the hips, touch the knees with fingertips then straighten up and shake it off.

In pre-season rankings, we started at number 12, which was ridiculous, so much so that coaches throughout the country made such an uproar that the next week we were dropped from the rankings altogether, even though we hadn't played a game. For the first time in anybody's memory, IU not only wasn't in the top 5 or 10, it wasn't even in the top 20. We were a nonentity. Unranked. Unknown. Shocking for a team that had racked up two national championships in recent years and been to the final four more than a dozen times. But something about being captain of an underdog team appealed to me. I wonder why.

The only snag was that once the season began, I wasn't in the starting lineup, which was kind of curious and fairly agitating to me. I hadn't seen any captain not be in the starting lineup. Even though I would get in games fairly early as a sub, it just didn't feel right. I tried to keep the persistent optimist front and center in my mind.

We lost the first game, then won a close one, and then shelled Michigan State 6-0. Next was a trip to South Bend, Indiana, and a match with University of Notre Dame, an in-state rival and obviously a big-name school, but we typically handled them pretty well. I still wasn't starting, and the concept kept gnawing at me.

We lost by a late penalty kick. I played very little. At least the coaches, who were particularly aggravated at that loss, couldn't blame me. On the bus ride back to Bloomington, Coach Yeagley made it very clear in some colorful word usage that was new to me that every spot on the team was up for grabs, that everyone better come to practice the next day ready to focus and play harder than they'd ever played.

We did, and the intensity at practice amped up a bit, which played right into my strengths. If I learned nothing else in my four-plus years,

I learned to compete like my life depended on it. I also could see that Coach Yeagley was trying new team combinations.

The next game a few days later was against Memphis State at home, and Coach Yeagley indeed did mix up the lineup a bit, inserting four new starters: Ken Godat, Jim Crockford, Juergen Sommer, and me at outside midfielder. This time, there was no cheering or slaps on the back or clapping. And, this time, I was ready to do what I do. No nerves about losing my position. No doubts about whether I belonged. Running through my system was a strange mix of calm and crackling energy. I was captain, and I was going to hit it head on. I may never have been as focused as I was when we walked up the hill to Armstrong Stadium.

Now, I'm smart enough to know that what happened in that game and over the next few weeks had little to do with my skills and more to do with my heart, and that what happened was a team effort in every sense of the phrase. But I also know that I was a significant part of what happened, and what happened was what some might call incredible.

We started by beating Memphis State 3-1, which really stoked Coach Yeagley's happy fire. Two days later, we clobbered Ohio State 5-0, with each goal scored by a different guy. Then we traveled to Bowling Green and beat them 3-1. The week after that, University of Akron, which was ranked No. 4 in the country, came to Bloomington. We knocked them off 1-0 on a goal by guess who? Big-timer Pete Stoyanovich.

We went to St. Louis in late September to play another gritty opponent, St. Louis University, a game that took on added importance because we had five guys on our roster from the St. Louis area. It started poorly for us, with the Billikens scoring a goal two minutes into the game.

That was the last time they would score. We found the back of the net three times and won the game 3-1.

We just kept rolling, appearing in the rankings for the first time, cracking the top 20. Miami University of Ohio came to Bloomington and probably wished they'd taken a wrong turn and gotten lost. We beat them 8-0, a game that had particular significance for me. I scored my first collegiate goal off a rebound from Stoyo in front of the goal. Fifteen minutes later, I scored again under almost the same circumstances—a rebound off the crossbar from Stoyo. The guy's so thoughtful of his teammate.

We moved up to number 8 in the rankings, headed to a tournament in Evansville, and won both games to claim the championship. In early October, it was Northwestern's turn. We torched them 7-0 and moved up to number 3 in the rankings.

Practices were loose and the coaches upbeat. "Casanova" by LeVert and "Back in the High Life Again" were blaring in the locker room. We genuinely liked each other and had achieved that rare balance of intensity and fun that made for magical chemistry. *Indianapolis Star* reporter Jim Uebelhoer sensed it.

"Camaraderie – which was painfully absent the past two years – is the main reason the Hoosiers are opening some eyes again this season," Jim wrote in the *Indianapolis Star* in October. Then he quoted Coach Yeagley:

"This team works very hard for each other," he said. "They put forth the effort to make each other look good. They enjoy playing together."

I guess I had learned a few leadership lessons over time.

I continued to focus very intently on team chemistry, and one of the main ingredients was making everybody a part of the mix, regardless of their contributions. Everybody moved goals and shagged soccer balls. I made it a point to talk to everybody all the time—coaches, trainers, the brightest stars on our team, and the lowliest 34th man. I reflected on my feelings and memories of being the 35th man and was darn sure that he, and everyone else on that roster, was going to feel as good about being a part of this team as our leading scorer did. I greeted everybody as they walked in the locker room and said goodbye to each one as they left. I talked constantly on the field, whether it was practices or games, always encouraging, affirming, and communicating everything that was unfolding in front of us. If I criticized, it was constructive and supportive. And, on campus, we were known as hard-working guys who had their fun but followed the rules.

My parents, Sherri, and the rest of my family were thrilled. They came to a bunch of games. We were writing letters back and forth with each other. Sherri's presence in particular was such a gift. Our practice of attending church anchored me. Meanwhile, she and her roommates became our biggest fans. I simply couldn't believe how fortunate I was in a hectic life that still had so much balance.

The hits kept coming. We knocked off Evansville and Cleveland State, then took flight to a tournament in Los Angeles where we beat San Diego State and UCLA to win the crown. We came back to the Midwest for our final game of the regular season and beat Wisconsin on the road, 2-0.

The team of unknowns had won 16 consecutive games, tying an IU record. Our national ranking? Numero uno, baby. By winning at Wisconsin and securing the nation's number-one ranking, we earned a bye in the first round of the NCAA tournament.

It was a phenomenal ride, unthinkable, really, when you remember where we'd started in August. We had role players. We had versatile stars. We had the song in our ears and chemistry flowing. We played really hard for each other and found whatever it took to win.

The kid who was never going to play at IU was captain of the best team in the country. I even scored six goals that year—third highest on the team.

Back in the high life, indeed. How about that for a dream come true?

****

Now that we had gotten this close, I figured why not extend the dream? Why not roll through the post-season and contribute another soccer national championship to IU's trophy case? That'd be a pretty cool way to finish my career. We kept track of the opening round of the tournament and saw that Clemson, a team that had squeaked into the tournament as a 24th seed, won in something of an upset and would be our next opponent. I have to admit that generated a little anxious flare-up in me. Clemson was a nemesis of sorts for us, beating IU in the 1984 NCAA championship game, beating us the year after that in a prominent tournament game at our place, and embarrassing us in a late-season game in 1986 that pretty much killed our post-season tournament chances.

They were dangerous, largely because winning one game in the tournament as a 24th seed was more success than anybody thought they would have achieved. For that reason, the Tigers were a loose bunch, playing all out with no pressure. Suddenly, I was nervous that our one-week layoff might stall our momentum.

When we jogged on the field for warm-ups on that gray, late November afternoon, more than 4,000 people in our home of Armstrong Stadium cheered. I think all of us guys felt a little extra pressure, different from the typical pre-game jitters. And, maybe we were a little foggy from our week off.

For whatever reason, from the opening kick, we were a little manic, firing shot after shot. Clemson withstood every push. Then we lost Sean Shapert, a critical guy who had a school record 18 assists, to a back injury. But big-game Stoyo stepped up—maybe he was the only one of us who was calm—and scored late in the first half to give us a 1-0 lead.

Clemson put the pressure on us the second half, winning balls all over the field and firing 13 shots. Two of those late in the game went into the goal. With about five minutes remaining, we penetrated deep and fired a shot—our only shot on goal that half—but the goalie caught up to it. Time expired. Season over way too soon.

Those moments immediately after the game seemed to unfold in slow motion and felt like some surreal, out-of-body experience. I was silent, sweat cooling on my body, wracked with pain and disbelief. I looked over at Stoyo, sitting on the bench in tears, upset that this would be our last game together.

We made our way to the locker room and changed in silence and tears. Coach Yeagley entered and told us this had been one of his proudest, most rewarding seasons. He admitted being disappointed but also never enjoying a year as much as he enjoyed this one. We shed more tears and finally went to dinner at a deli, rehashing game moments, doing the old, woulda-coulda-shoulda, engaging in group therapy. Then, grudgingly we all went home and tried to get sleep.

The next day, I dragged myself through classes and headed to the locker room where all of us were going to clear our lockers and turn in our gear. I was pulling stuff from my stall when teammate John Trask walked over and asked to see my practice ball. He took it from my hand, signed it, and passed it to another guy. In a couple of minutes, all 15 to 20 guys in the locker room had signed it. I'd never seen that before, and I don't know how to express exactly how it felt. It was so powerful in part because it was spontaneous and obviously heartfelt. I was caught off guard and couldn't hold back the tears. I had so much love for the guys in that room.

We scattered for Thanksgiving break. Clemson, that upstart team of loose underdogs, surprised a lot of people and won the national championship 2-0 over San Diego State—yeah, the same team we'd beaten near the end of the regular season.

I graduated in December, moved back home to Carmel, and went to work for the family's soccer retail business, Soccer Unlimited. We opened a second store in Indianapolis, and I managed the place. Sherri and I continued seeing each other, and she graduated in May. Stoyo ended up focusing on football only and got drafted by the Miami Dolphins. He went on to become one of the National Football League's most accurate and consistent placekickers in a 12-year career. Although he lives in Michigan, we still talk all the time.

IU's next soccer season started, and I attended every home game, went to practices occasionally, and kept in touch with Coach Yeagley and a couple players. They picked up where we left off, had a really strong regular season, and entered the NCAA tournament ranked number nine. Four games later, they were ranked number one because they won the national championship 1-0 over Howard University at IU's Armstrong Stadium. Sherri, a bunch of friends, and I were in the stands, and when the Hoosiers won, I thought for an instant about what might have been one year earlier, but was too overwhelmed with joy for our guys for reaching the high life again. That's all I had room for in my heart.

A couple of weeks later, I got an invitation in the mail to the soccer team's championship banquet, which was a surprise. It's a pretty intimate affair for players, coaches, families, a few university people, and heavy-hitting soccer program supporters. Not alums. I was pretty pumped.

Sherri and I drove down to Bloomington on a frosty night, greeted a bunch of friends in the glittering ballroom, and, after a while sat down to a delicious dinner. I looked around the room and noticed the only other soccer alum among the 70 or so people attending was Bruce Killough, co-captain with me from last year.

This year's co-captain, Herb Haller, started the speeches by talking about the wonderful season, saying how fulfilling it was to bring IU back to the top, how supportive the entire environment was this year. Then he paused and looked at me.

"The only regret I have is that the guys who had the most to do with this championship run, Whitey and Bruce, weren't on the team," Herb said.

People started cheering. I sat there, stunned, trying to suppress the humility, gratitude, and overwhelming emotion flowing through me.

Next was assistant coach Joe Kelly, who said the same thing, adding that it was a shame Bruce and I didn't get a championship ring. People broke into applause again. Then assistant coach Don Rawson stood and said the same thing about the impact we had on the program. I glanced at Bruce, a guy I really admired, and I was just as excited for him as I was for me. Even though Bruce had become a back-up goalkeeper early in our final season, he'd remained a leader off the field, never letting his personal disappointment at being a nonstarter detract from that leadership. He was a crucial piece.

Then came Coach Yeagley, who reiterated what the others had said about Bruce and me. My biggest doubter and critic now was my loudest cheerleader. I came to find out that he'd sent my parents a letter months earlier saying I was "one of the finest leaders [he had] been fortunate enough to be associated with."

Life can be weirdly cool at times.

While we rolled up Highway 37 toward Carmel after the festivities, I thought how different that night's trip was from the first trip I'd taken to IU to meet Coach Yeagley. I thought about all that I'd experienced on a five-year odyssey. I found myself wondering what would have happened if I hadn't roomed with Stolly and Keith, if I'd transferred to Southern Indiana, if my little champ of a fifth metatarsal had failed me, if I hadn't become close friends with Stoyo, fallen in love with Sherri, been named captain by Coach Yeagley. I thought about how I'd changed and grown into a leader from a kid who started out only wanting to play soccer at the premier college team in the country.

As uncomfortable as this is for me to say, I'm proud of what I accomplished. I learned invaluable lessons about discipline, team structure, pushing myself, and leadership and the commitment to winning. They are lessons that set the tone of my personal and professional life.

But, I find another aspect of the journey just as fascinating. The odyssey really was about this thing we had built, and it makes me think that life and leadership is really about personal accomplishments to advance the team or even society, not about advancing the self. "Winning" in the conventional sense is a by-product of that approach. It's how authentic champions are made and legacies built. That's where true fulfillment is and where *philotimo* thrives.

My college experience was pretty extraordinary and, if you want to read the full story, make sure to pick up the book I wrote about it, *To Chase a Dream*, published by Meyer & Meyer Sport.

That experience also taught me a thing or two about leadership and life. I've synthesized those over the years to a few principles that I lean on to this day, personally and professionally. They might inspire you, too, or help you inspire someone else.

1. **Set attainable goals.** Decide where you want to be. Make it reachable but a real stretch. Write them down; write down why you want to get there and exactly how you're going to get there. Place them someplace where you'll see them every day. You might even want to compose a collage of photos and phrases from magazines that depict that objective. When your head hits the pillow every night, say a little affirmative prayer. And, don't worry too much about how or when you want to reach your goal. Just make sure you're moving in that direction, even if it's baby steps on crutches.

2. **Have dreams.** This is pie-in-the-sky stuff, fantasy. President of the United States, your own tropical island, hitting a home run in the World Series, playing lead guitar in front of thousands, winning a Nobel Prize or Academy Award. Regularly picture yourself in the position of achieving that dream. Enjoy that sensation. It plants the seed, and once you plant the seed, if you nourish it, you might surprise yourself and watch it grow into something really cool. Help let it happen.

3. **Surround yourself with supportive, enthusiastic, can-do people**. And be one of those people. Pretty self-explanatory. Be a good listener, a kind friend who is there for others and generous in all ways. Live out loud with positive energy and don't be surprised if it comes right back to you.

4. **Believe in yourself.** You must know you can do whatever you set out to do. Balance hard work with a peaceful mind and incredible desire.

5. **Persevere.** Embrace the journey even if it doesn't end where you wanted. Be willing to endure the rough patches, which can be longer and rougher than you think. Know that failure is a better learning and growing experience than success, and, when you do fail, absorb the lesson, adapt, and move forward. Understand that patient persistence is the key and that a healthy sense of humor, especially the ability to laugh at yourself, is vital.

6. **Rely on your faith.** Prayer is a very powerful thing. It is energy. It heals. It comforts. It gives courage. I lean on God throughout my day, every day, for the all-consuming concerns and smallest anxieties, for everything. It starts and ends with Him. When you have done all that you can, relinquish control and rely on your faith. The sooner you place your full trust in Him and thank Him for all the abundance you have in life, the sooner and more often you will walk through life with more prosperity, surer footing, calmer mind, and loving heart.

# CHAPTER 3
# COACHES' EPILOGUE

After *To Chase a Dream* was published, it sparked a few spontaneous reunions of the Indiana University soccer family, and it is a family. Players, coaches, and their loved ones would turn out for book events and at conferences or other places where I'd speak. After I'd wrap up, a bunch of us would go out, tell old stories, and laugh until the wee hours. It was such a wonderful outcome of writing the book, one I hadn't anticipated fully.

One of the guys who showed up a few times was Coach Yeagley, who provided the introduction for *To Chase a Dream*. At a couple of events, he publicly spoke very graciously about my time at IU, calling me one of the greatest leaders he'd ever coached and expressing how powerful and instructive my journey had been for him, which, frankly, surprised me.

I've done a fair amount of coaching youth soccer, which I absolutely love, and coaches throughout my life have been a strong, formative presence. They are in any athlete's life. I've also paid close attention to coaches I've met or seen work, trying to pick up signs of their philosophies and strategies of leadership and determine how they form their leadership codes.

I had the rare opportunity to experience Coach Yeagley's approach firsthand for an extended period. It was simply one of the greatest experiences of my life. The time I spent playing for him, being a part of that great tradition, was invaluable, on and off the field. The winning culture, family atmosphere, and overall experience were life lessons wrapped into four-and-a-half years, lessons I never could have learned in the classroom alone.

Almost 25 years later, I had an equally rare experience of watching another coach for only a few days, but those were telling days that gave me enormous insight. That coach was Mike Krzyzewski, leader of powerhouse Duke University men's basketball team.

Both of those experiences with these two coaches, though very different, were really illuminating. I thought I'd share distilled versions of them—one from a Steak 'n Shake in Bloomington, Indiana, on a rainy Saturday morning; the other from the pressure-cooker that is the NCAA men's basketball Final Four. I hope you'll find both instructive.

Coach Yeagley retired from IU in 2003 after a 40-year career in which he won six national championships and achieved an overall record of 544 wins, 101 losses, and 45 ties to become the all-time NCAA leader in victories. He was named National Soccer Coaches Association of America Coach of the Year six times, Big Ten Coach of the Year eight times, and inducted into the US Soccer Federation Hall of Fame and the National Soccer Coaches Association of America Hall of Fame. And here's an interesting factoid that gets at his ability to achieve greatness: He is the only person to play on a high school state championship team and an NCAA championship team and coach an NCAA championship squad.

That kind of leadership, for obvious reasons, intrigues me. And, even though I stayed in touch with Coach Yeagley over the years, I hadn't really gotten a chance to talk with him about his own leadership journey, how he built his leadership philosophy. So I called him, and we met at Steak 'n Shake.

At 76, he looked great; he still had that sparkle in his eye and a quick smile. We got a small booth toward the back and talked for more than an hour. It was wonderful and a bit rare. Coach Yeagley, in his humble way, generally preferred to talk about others rather than himself.

To fully understand his achievements, it's important to appreciate where Coach Yeagley's journey started. He learned to play soccer on the playgrounds of Myerstown, Pennsylvania, a small community about 90 miles northwest of Philadelphia. He went on to star at Myerstown High School and play on its state championship team. He continued playing at what is now West Chester University where he was on the 1961 national championship team.

From there, it was grad school at University of Pittsburgh. Then he landed in Bloomington in 1963 as a physical education instructor and supervisor—not coach—of the men's club soccer team, which was just like it sounded, a pretty informal collection of guys who played other schools in what was a notch or two above pick-up games. He was 23 years old and traveled that far west because he was told that converting the club team to a varsity sport was possible. He wanted to be a pioneer in the game. At his first team meeting shortly after arriving on campus, he got a sense of the challenge facing him in making that conversion.

"One of the big concerns," Coach Yeagley recalled, "and there were only about eight or nine people who showed up at the first club meeting, was where are the trips so we can plan our parties?"

He laughed, recalling that moment. It would take him a decade to transform the club to a NCAA varsity team, mostly because IU's athletic department didn't want men's soccer to be a varsity sport, regardless of what had been communicated to him when he was weighing job offers. That's another interesting story about a different brand of leadership.

He immediately changed his status from supervisor to coach and told the guys that the objective was to become a varsity team and that they were going to run the team in every way possible as a varsity sport. Commitment to the team was going to be essential.

"It was a bit of a tug-of-war with some of them who had been there and didn't necessarily want to do the types of things you need to do to be successful on a varsity program," Coach Yeagley told me. "That was a challenge, and it became a little frustrating. But eventually, the players bought in and worked very hard."

How did he change that culture? He set goals that he actually wrote out and explained how those goals would be achieved. Then he sought player-leaders who agreed, guys who wanted to excel and who wanted to hold players accountable. They immediately imposed team rules that matched those of varsity sports: Nobody who would be academically ineligible to play a varsity sport would play club soccer; all players had to be full-time students.

It may have been considered a little forceful these days, but I'm not going to be too judgmental more than a half century later. This was the early 1960s, a much simpler time. And, his strategy worked. The team's level of play improved steadily. They became very successful in the club leagues and regularly would knock off varsity teams from other schools, something that IU's players took a great deal of pride in. Players also turned out to be great promoters, handing out schedules in dorms and hanging fliers across campus announcing the date and time of the next game.

Students actually started turning out to watch games. Crowds had as many as 2,000 people. The club team became so popular, in fact, that the student body petitioned to have soccer converted to a varsity sport, and the Athletic Department signaled it was going to approve the concept.

"But I got called in [by the athletic director, the director of intramurals, and the men's dean of students], and they said, 'This is not what club's about,'" Coach Yeagley recalled them saying. "'You gotta back off and treat it more as a social entity.' We had a come to Jesus meeting, and I almost left at that point."

IU hadn't added a varsity sport for 25 years, and administrators were less than interested in taking on the additional work and money a new sport would require. The athletic director told Coach Yeagley he wouldn't get a dime; the relationship between the two became pretty strained.

But Coach Yeagley decided against leaving, and he realized he wasn't going to get what he wanted by force. So, he swallowed his pride and adopted an approach that might best be summed up as the old saying that you catch more flies with honey than vinegar.

He got to know the writers and editors of Bloomington's paper and the student newspaper and the local radio stations, and he made a point of taking them to breakfast or meeting them for coffee. He sought out faculty who were members of the Athletics Committee, which was responsible for recommending the addition of a new sport, and befriended them. He established a friendly relationship with former IU president, Herman Wells, an almost mythic and beloved leader known for his energy, empathy, charm, and communication skills in a career at IU that spanned 63 years between his role as president and chancellor. Wells liked soccer for its international appeal and was a key advocate.

Coach Yeagley also developed his friendship with Bill Armstrong, executive director and president of the Indiana University Foundation, the school's fundraising arm. He turned out to be a big supporter in a number of ways. In fact, that's why the soccer stadium is named for him. The team also was lucky to have the IU student body president as one of its members.

All those people got onboard, and when the Athletics Committee recommended soccer become a varsity sport in 1973, the athletic director was, according to Coach Yeagley, thrilled. He told Coach that he'd wanted the sport to be a varsity activity for some time. He had a funny way of showing it for those 10 years, though.

That's one aspect of leadership that I hadn't given much thought to before our chat at Steak 'n Shake. But I think it's worth pointing out that Coach Yeagley had a very clear vision of what he wanted, and when his approach to attain that vision ran into a brick wall, he could have quit and gone somewhere that was more receptive to what he wanted to do or browbeat the athletic department into submission. Instead, he rethought his strategy and found a way.

Rather than pounding the brick wall with a battering ram, he was able to foster relationships with and persuade people all around the brick wall with the why—why soccer as a varsity sport was such a great idea. He generated the right vibe, the good karma, whatever you want to call it. Instead of forcing a reluctant athletic department, he enlightened people over there to the obvious conclusion and that momentum was building; that it would be fun, easy, almost heroic to jump aboard and be part of something bigger; to give people what they'd wanted.

By doing that, Coach Yeagley turned the wall into a bridge.

When he got the phone call notifying him that men's soccer would become a varsity sport, he said he felt very relieved and still had some disbelief that it actually happened. Today, he said, he thinks very fondly back on those 10 years when the team was a club. He thinks about how they had to do so much on their own. "I think that was a big part of our family-building and pride in the uniform that we took forward," he said.

Like every coach, he relied on the coaching philosophies he'd experienced as a player. And, Coach Yeagley had a pretty rare experience of excelling under two completely different types of people: Barney Hoffman, his high school coach, and Mel Lorback, who coached him in college.

Barney, who also had worked as a playground supervisor, taught Coach Yeagley how to play the game as a kid as well as the passion of the game, the beautiful part of the game. "Everybody loved him," Coach Yeagley recalled. "He was a role model of total respect, and he loved the game."

"Mel was a military guy. Short guy. Napoleon type," Coach Yeagley told me. Mel was obsessed with every detail, with organization and preparation. "That's how I learned how important it was to be prepared and pay attention to the little things, the small details."

Coach said Mel was a little egotistical and that his motivational tactics directed at his players were negativity and fear. It was too much for him, and he admitted he almost quit his freshman year at West Chester. In fact, Coach Yeagley told me, he didn't much care for Mel while playing for him.

He added, "I learned through that, and we won. But he was so different from Barney, who was compassionate and humanistic and loving. With Mel, it was, 'God, you better do this or you're in deep doo-doo,' you know?"

Except that a funny thing happened after Coach Yeagley graduated.

"He felt like I was almost like a son to him," coach said of Mel. "We became very close, and I realized under that veneer of tough, mean, negative was a very warm person. But that was his insecurity. Even though he had a strong ego, I felt that he was an insecure guy."

Coach Yeagley kept in touch with both men until they passed, taking the best from his playing experience with them and seeking their advice. Throughout that time, he blended it with his own personality, and he evolved.

When I asked him about his overall approach to leadership, he gave me several elements: Know your personal goals; have a plan and believe in yourself and what you're doing; be unafraid to be challenged or to adapt to the times, but stay true to your core values; make sure the game's fun; and emphasize the positive aspects of players. Have a passion for what you're doing.

"You have to be genuine, and they have to see it," he said. "They have to respect that, and they have to want to buy into that. I think a strong leader exudes that. And, a strong leader wants to surround himself with strong people. An insecure leader doesn't want to be challenged. A strong leader wants people who maybe are even better at some things than he is, and he feels comfortable with that."

He said leaders need to be fiercely competitive. Then he talked about his emphasis on performance rather than results, which I found interesting for a guy with so much winning on his résumé.

His thinking was that individuals need to focus on pursuing perfection in their performance and the tangible results—whether it's wins, booming sales numbers, high test scores, or what have you—will follow.

"My approach is you achieve excellence through performance ignited by motivation," Coach Yeagley said. "Like Vince Lombardi said, 'Perfection is unachievable, but if you chase it hard enough, you just might find excellence.' I strove for excellence, and motivation is crucial."

So much of what he told me came down to the psychological, the internal motivation. Coach Yeagley talked about building relationships, creating a family atmosphere, understanding the emotional side of athletes, and nurturing trust and a close relationship with those athletes. He said great leaders never allow adversity and low morale to hang around.

"Good leaders, winners, work through adversity very quickly and get back on track," Coach said. "They don't let the players mire in it and drag them lower. That's for losers."

One fundamental in his leadership mosaic is finding people who already have at least a few of the right character components—people who want to work really hard, play with integrity, and communicate. Over time, he said, he learned to pass over potential recruits who had crazy talent, instead going after guys who might grade at a lower skill level but had heart and character.

"Guys who developed over three, four years—the Whiteys of the world—we probably had more of those at IU than most programs," he said, "and those are the guys who, when they do make it to where they can play, have so much pride and understanding instilled with the winning qualities that they can overcome that highly talented, God-given-talented player."

Over that three or four years, Coach Yeagley would work to mold that attitude. He is a strong advocate of the theory that performance follows attitude.

"As a coach, you need to shape their attitude. I always used to shape thinking from fear to courage, from anxiety to confidence. That was always a big part of my approach."

And the clearest indication that his leadership was working occurred when his student-athletes took ownership and held each other accountable on and off the field. It's very rare that you get an entire team that bonds that way, something I know well from my own coaching experience. But when you do orchestrate that, great things usually happen.

For him, he started with taking ownership way back in 1963. As a club team, the guys had no real support from the Athletic Department. They had to do everything themselves; even Coach Yeagley's wife, Marilyn, got deeply involved, cooking team meals and washing uniforms. The guys drove their own cars to games, piling players inside. On the road, they'd eat at the family homes of players. They'd even line their own fields. That spirit carried over when it became a varsity team.

The key to all of it, he said, was being able to find a way to get a person to self-motivate, to be personally inspired. "Lighting that fire, that burning desire, is the truest motivation," he said.

You've got to build trust as a leader, and Coach worked very hard at that. He really enjoyed when he'd get a knock at the door and a player was standing there asking to have a talk with him. Sometimes, players would reveal their most personal secrets or issues, from school and family problems to difficulties with girlfriends and more.

"Many times, the coach becomes closer to an individual than most anyone," he told me. Research, in fact, supports that statement. "I had players come to me with situations they didn't take to their parents. I had more than one player open up to me about their sexuality, something they had never talked to anyone else about. And, when a trust or a feeling between a coach and a player is that strong, you have a chance to affect the life of an individual more than having them become a good soccer player."

Coach loved that part of the job.

It's true that by gaining a clearer, fuller understanding of all his players, a leader starts to see what makes them tick, what drives them, and how he, as a coach, manager, or supervisor, can push the buttons to get the highest possible performance from individuals. Some may view that as manipulative, but that's a very limited perspective. The great leaders understand never to betray that trust, but instead use elements of it to bring out the highest performance to help that individual become his or her best, which is incredibly fulfilling for that individual. Don't we all want to experience our personal best as consistently as possible? Don't we all want to understand how to do that?

****

Another person who clearly understands this leadership stuff is Coach K at Duke. For those unfamiliar with his story, Mike Krzyzewski was born in 1947 in Chicago to a father who was an elevator operator and a mother who worked as a cleaning lady. He shared a two-story home with extended family in a working-class Polish neighborhood on the city's north side, and he was an outstanding athlete, especially in basketball.

So outstanding that he was offered a scholarship to West Point by a fiery young coach named Bobby Knight. Mike was team captain and later worked as an assistant coach to Coach Knight at Indiana University. In 1975, Coach K started his college head coaching career at his alma mater, West Point, before taking the Duke University job in 1980.

Since then, things have gone pretty well for Duke Basketball and Coach K.

Duke men's teams have won five national championships. In addition, Coach K has won six gold medals leading the USA Men's National Team.

Entering the 2016-17 season, he had won 1,043 games and lost 321, including a 970-262 record at Duke.

He has received National Coach of the Year honors 12 times.

Among players who've completed four years of eligibility at Duke, 98 percent have graduated.

In addition, he and his family are extremely active in the community, especially in campaigns against drunk driving and drug abuse. Among other efforts, Coach K and his wife, Mickie, have served as co-chairs of a telethon that raises money for Duke Children's Hospital & Health Center.

In his spare time, he's written several books on the topic of leadership, all of which are illuminating.

For me, one of the most powerful is *Leading With the Heart: Successful Strategies for Basketball, Business, and Life,* published in 2000 by Warner Books. It's full of thoughtful nuggets such as encouraging other teammates to mentor younger teammates; setting goals that focus more on strengthening the team than on personal achievement; confronting simply means meeting the truth head on; if one of us isn't doing well, none of us is doing well; the worse the crisis, the more people tend to act as individuals rather than as members of a team; learning your limits then trying to extend them; when you're a leader, somebody somewhere will be trying to take you down; remembering to enjoy the moment and the achievement; and making time for building, nurturing, and sustaining relationships.

I got a taste of this legend over a fairly intense five days in 2010 when a friend, Bob Woerner, and I volunteered as site coordinators for Indiana Sports Corporation. The non-profit Sports Corp promotes Indianapolis as host of sporting events across a wide spectrum from

18 Olympic team trials and the 1987 Pan American Games to six Big Ten football championships and seven NCAA Men's Final Fours.

Bob and I were assigned to host Duke's basketball team at Lucas Oil Stadium. I've had the privilege of being a site coordinator to many, many college basketball coaches and their teams as they rolled through Indianapolis for Big Ten Conference tournaments, NCAA Regionals, and all Final Fours. None have made quite the impression that Duke did.

As site coordinators, we're part ambassador, part concierge, and part go-fer. Essentially, we're the guys they can turn to when and if they need something or have a question. Bob had been a site coordinator for several years prior to me serving in that role, and he epitomized why Indianapolis is so successful at hosting events: their great volunteer base. Bob showed me the ropes, and we made a pretty effective tandem. He would focus on overall team needs. I would commit to making sure the head coach was all set. It made for a great approach, and the players and staff always felt welcomed and had the necessary coverage.

Any time our respective team or coach is at the stadium, so are we. When I was told I'd be hosting Duke, I was really intrigued. My first encounter with them was a telling example of Coach K's leadership.

It came on Thursday night. One of my roles as site coordinator is to stand in the tunnel of the stadium to greet the team as it exits its bus. My first day, I was at my post when Duke's bus rolled up. I'd done this dozens of times for dozens of coaches and their teams. Every single time, the bus would pull up, the door would open, and out would step the coach followed by the players.

Not with Coach K and Duke.

When Duke's bus stopped and the doors opened, I could see inside. Coach K was sitting in front. He stood, but remained near the bus driver. As each player passed him on their way out the door, Coach K hugged the guy. He waited until every player was off the bus, and then he exited. I'd never seen that before and, as small of a gesture as it was, it made a pretty powerful, immediate impact on me and set the stage for the following days.

Throughout that time, Coach K was respectful, consistent, and very present with everyone he dealt with, from reporters and volunteers to his staff, family, and, of course, his players, who also conducted themselves with class. Having that ability under such high-stress, frenzied circumstances was astonishing. He had this aura of calm focus while everything else was pretty tense and swirling.

We chatted for about five minutes that Thursday night, just basic stuff about me and my role. I told him some of the details about how things unfold, and that was it. Next morning, we connected again, and he remembered my name, asked how my night went, and how things were going for me. Most of all, he was sincere about it. Just remembering my name was unique among coaches I've dealt with, but his genuine effort to take the time to chat with me in a very personable manner was another of those small insights into his character. He didn't have to even acknowledge the blip on his screen that was me. Nobody would have faulted him.

I hung out, which is part of my job in this role, and watched Duke practice in case the team needed anything. It was fascinating to observe the dynamic at work while Coach K and his staff ran the guys through drills, scrimmages, and other parts of the practice. It was a rare mix of precision, intensity, and purpose, but the team also was loose and confident. They were going into a pressure cooker of a semi-final game against West Virginia, and the team still managed to enjoy themselves. Coach K made sure of it.

That day, we visited for a few more minutes beyond small talk. Again, his ability to be present in the moment was uncanny. I found out how strong his Catholic faith is, among other themes of his life. When we were getting ready to go our separate ways after practice, I wished him a happy Good Friday. I could tell that registered with him, that it meant something. He nodded and said that was pretty cool, that he'd never really had someone express that to him while on the road at previous Final Fours.

The next day, game day, I was pretty pumped to see how Duke would perform. I waited for the team bus to arrive in the tunnel and watched the same process unfold—Coach K hugging each player before they got off the bus, making him the last one to exit. Then another very cool thing happened.

Mickie was there in the tunnel standing next to me. When Coach K got off the bus, he grabbed his bag, reached for Mickie's hand, and they walked hand-in-hand from the bus to the locker room entrance. Once they got to the door, they embraced for a minute, exchanged some words, and went their separate ways—Coach K to the locker room, Mickie to her seat in the stadium. Again, it may seem like a small gesture, but to me it was an extremely meaningful reminder of the couple's priorities: presence and life balance.

Duke won on Saturday night, beating West Virginia 78-57 and advancing to the championship. After the game, at the suggestion of Bob, I mentioned to one of his assistants that, with the next day being Easter, I'd be happy to serve communion to Coach K, if he was interested. I'm a Eucharistic minister at my parish and serve communion there, but it's pretty rare for me to serve what's known as homebound communion. This seemed like an appropriate moment to at least make the offer.

The assistant coach emerged from the locker room about a minute later and said Coach K would really appreciate that. The next morning, we found a quiet corner of the locker room. I laid out my Rosary and holy water, lit a candle, and served him communion. It was a very moving experience for both of us and gave us a chance to talk afterward about our faith. My wife, Sherri—that's right, my college sweetheart became my lovely bride—made the moment that much more special by packing Easter baskets of chocolates and other goodies for Coach K's grandchildren who had traveled to Indianapolis for the Final Four. He was genuinely grateful. Later, Duke's athletic director told me no one had ever offered gestures like that to Coach K while on the road.

I don't know that I've ever had a more powerful 15 minutes of conversation, and here he was, a day before his team played one of the most important games in the history of the program. Again, Coach K was incredibly focused on the moment.

By Monday morning when we reconnected, Coach K had me feeling like I was part of the team. I never even entered the locker room with the team or attended any meetings. He just showed such sincere warmth toward me that by early afternoon, I was pumped and ready to pull on a uniform if they needed a vertically challenged, 46-year-old suburban dad of three to hit the hard court. I felt almost exactly like I had about my team 25 years earlier at IU. Coach K made that happen.

As many college basketball fans recall, Duke won the game that night, a heart-pounding, close contest in which Butler University's Gordon Hayward fired a half-court shot at the buzzer that hit the rim and narrowly missed. Final score: Duke 61, Butler 59. The Blue Devils had earned their fourth men's basketball championship. It was, of course, pandemonium, but Coach K was able to balance his joy with humility and kept his focus on the team, always on the team.

He accepted the trophy, did all the interviews, cut down his piece of the net, and went into the locker room with the guys. I stood outside. A few minutes later, Coach K came out, handed me a national championship cap, thanked me for everything, and then scooted back inside. A few weeks later, I got a note in the mail from him thanking me again.

That's a leader who has a strong sense of *philotimo*. No wonder he's one of the most successful coaches in basketball history.

I learned a lot in that brief time with Coach K, lessons about team building I use to this day in sports, business, and my personal life.

The great thing about leadership as a coach is that you can lead at any level, whether you're coaching a recreational third-grade football team or a Super Bowl-winning team. And in that role, no matter the level or setting, you have the chance to change lives for the better, instilling values, providing an exemplary role model, maybe simply giving the extra little encouragement that could make the difference for a child, teen, or adult.

I've coached youth soccer for many years, beginning with kindergarten recreation soccer all the way through pretty competitive club teams of kids in their late teens and have enjoyed every moment of the journey. I've done my best to embrace the most effective leadership qualities I've absorbed over the years from people like Coach Yeagley and Coach K and from my own experiences as captain of various teams I played on.

Now, I would never put my name in the same sentence as Coach Yeagley or Coach K, but I do embrace the opportunities that are in front of me, regardless of the stage, from my back yard to the most competitive fields in the country.

One of my more memorable experiences along those lines was coaching one of my daughter's club teams from the time the girls were 12 to 13 until they were 17. We began our journey together as a team ranked 54th in the state. Not so great.

But, having played for some outstanding coaches in my life, I knew a fair amount about the powerful, positive impact they can have on their players' lives. I also knew that, today, the practice and game fields are the only places where players do not have their cell phones, the only places where coaches have their undivided attention, and I thought that dynamic gave me a chance to be more than just a soccer coach to these young ladies.

I wanted them to know that, while soccer was the common bond we shared, their lives outside of soccer were equally, if not more, important. Throughout those years, I stressed the basics I've talked about throughout this book: belief in themselves, belief in each other, hard work, unity, trust, and optimism, to name a few. But the thing that might have had the single greatest impact, in terms of overall success, was something we called "Reflection Monday."

We would spend the first 15 to 20 minutes of practice every Monday— without cell phones—talking about life, about the girls' weekends, about school, about their social lives, their successes, their challenges, and their dreams. We basically talked about everything *except* soccer. Some girls spoke a lot and often. Some girls never spoke at all. We did not have an agenda and never put a time limit on the discussion if I felt the discussion needed to continue.

It was pretty cool to watch the impact spread through the team's personality over the weeks and months and years. Sometimes as coaches, we place way too much emphasis on the sport itself— executing our drills, pushing our techniques, lecturing and lecturing players about this or that—and we don't really allow the human element to exist and take root.

What happened with "Reflection Monday" was that just by carving out a little time for non-soccer talk, we created transparency, open communication, and an incredible trust that manifested itself in the girls' pretty phenomenal commitment to each other in games and more importantly in their off-the-field lives. They learned to empathize and love each other. It opened their eyes, minds, and hearts and that made for a very strong, authentic bond. As the season progressed, the girls began showing up 15, 20, 30 minutes early for Monday practices so they could extend our reflection time without cutting into the training session. Pretty powerful stuff.

Then you know what happened? In our third year together, they won the Indiana state championship.

But, see, the important thing to remember here is that our coaching, including our "Reflection Mondays," wasn't all that much about winning. It was about building something bigger, about imparting experiences and wisdom that are valuable in life. Winning was a happy byproduct.

I believe that our communication, trust, and bond were huge parts of the growth of every one of those little girls who became young women. In fact, when I run into one of them now and we have a few minutes to chat, they'll tell me how much they enjoyed the experience, and they almost never say anything about the championship or the wins. It's everything else that made a lasting impact. Sometimes they don't even have to tell me. I can see the expression of genuine appreciation in their eyes, and then I get goosebumps. The real truth is that I was the one who benefitted from their efforts. They gave me the gift of an incredibly memorable, uplifting journey.

It's a pretty great feeling, a *philotimo* kind of feeling, and I'm so grateful we were able to play those roles in each other's lives.

# ■ CHAPTER 4
# TRUSTING TRANSPARENCY

## ■ LEADERSHIP AS A PARENT

As well as sport distills lessons of leadership, business can make them pretty messy. An enormous number of leadership lessons exist in business, but we often have to slog through fairly complicated, real-world scenarios to find them. Anyone who has worked in business for a few years knows that.

The rewards typically are much less glorious and visceral than intercepting a pass and running it back for a touchdown, scoring a game-winning goal with three seconds left on the clock, hitting a home run to win the game, or sinking a three-point buzzer beater. But leadership lessons learned in business often can be more enduring than those snapshots.

And, sometimes the lessons of business are about something more than how to run a private enterprise better. In unexpected ways, sometimes the lessons of business show you how to run your life better. In what was my most painful business experience, I learned how to be a better husband and father.

As I mentioned earlier, my mom started a business way back in 1982. At the time, she had four soccer-playing sons and found it next to impossible to find gear for us in and around Indianapolis. After routinely driving to Chicago to find gear, she realized the chances were pretty strong that many, many parents and players in central Indiana faced similar challenges.

That thinking led to the creation of Soccer Unlimited, which was born in a pretty cramped space that had 1,000 square feet of retail in Carmel. It was not exactly your ideal location for a store. Customers had to enter a door, turn right at the end of one hall, and turn left at the end of another hall to finally enter the store through a small door. I guess you could call it a true "destination" retail location. As modest as it was at the outset, Soccer Unlimited was another example of my parents' view of leadership and life: Chase what you believe in, particularly if it serves the greater good.

The store carried footwear, shin guards, shorts, t-shirts, socks, and soccer balls—the essentials to outfit a player. After a few years, she added a team sales division that provided uniforms and equipment to middle schools, high schools, colleges, and clubs.

From the outset, my mom established our unwritten mission statement: Treat everyone who comes in the store as if they were walking into our home. She hit speed bumps, and the learning curve was steep, but my mom is incredibly optimistic, resolute, enthusiastic, resilient, and quick learning. She also has a very deep well of energy. On top of all those, she is probably the most genuine "people person" I know. People love being around her.

Those characteristics worked really well in a retail setting. They work well in just about any setting when you think about it. Within five years, she had established a core business strategy, philosophy, and customer base. As we boys got older, we gravitated toward working at the store.

After he graduated from Michigan State, Pete joined the company in the finance department. Danny graduated from Indiana a couple of years later and became retail general manager. He and Pete then came up with a great idea: Soccer Unlimited Summer Camps. Danny was camp director, and Pete helped organize and run them. The camps served players throughout central Indiana and drew about 1,000 kids every year for more than 15 years. They not only offered outstanding training and development for players, but also served as a terrific marketing tool for everything Soccer Unlimited stood for.

After graduating from IU, I had the chance to go to work full time at Soccer Unlimited, just like my brothers had before me. But I was unsure. It's no secret that family businesses can be tough, that they are not for the weak of heart. They become much more personal than working for a company that has no family connection to you. The work spills into almost every element of your life and family relationships. It's definitely not the kind of work you can leave at the office when you turn off the light and head out the door. I'd seen some of those difficulties play out, even though I was removed from the daily operations by being away at school.

One important distinction was that even though we had our disagreements, we made a conscious decision in our family business that the word "family" comes before "business." Through our ups and downs, that concept stayed central to our approach. Our most important value and highest priority was keeping our family strong.

I considered taking a shot at working for an agricultural chemical company, a job that probably would have been better paying at the outset than going to work at Soccer Unlimited. But I love soccer. The opportunity to give back to a game that continued to mean so much to me—and give to the larger community—was a powerful draw, as was the energy my parents and brothers brought to the business. I decided to follow that instead of the money.

By the time I joined the company, Soccer Unlimited was flourishing, and we'd opened a second location. My job was to manage it. That same year, my dad retired from his 27-year career in corporate America and joined the business, making it a real family affair. The five of us—my parents, Pete, Danny, and I—grew even closer and created so many great experiences while we all worked hard to build Soccer Unlimited. We had some tough times. What new business doesn't? But the overwhelming memories I have of those days and nights are of laughter and fulfillment. It was priceless, and I think all of us know we'll never have anything quite like it again in our lives.

A few years later, U.S. Soccer named us the #1 Soccer Specialty Retail Store in the nation. We were beyond thrilled. What started as the classic mom-and-pop store had become a model for soccer retail outlets across the country. And, the thing that made it so powerful for us was that though the award was based on revenue, of course, it was also based on service, selection, and customer satisfaction. We knew we weren't the largest soccer store, but that was okay because our reputation in those other areas made us prouder than how big we could get. And, we were convinced that our success was almost entirely due to our strengths in how we treated our employees and served our customers.

By this point, I had really embraced all components of the business—retail, team accounts, and camps—and found I loved business in general. I loved the challenge of growing a business, training employees, serving customers, and making a difference in the community. I loved it so much that, as my parents got older and my brothers became more involved in coaching, I ended up buying their shares. It was all amicable. I then became the sole owner of Soccer Unlimited.

It was a step I felt more than ready for, and I enjoyed waking up every day, meeting the challenges head on, and seizing the opportunities. In a few years, I grew the company to five retail locations, an accomplishment I was proud of. But I also routinely found myself in a tight financial bind. Inventory and overhead consumed most of our resources. While we were generating millions of dollars in revenue, we lacked resources that larger companies benefit from—resources such as hiring practices, employee training programs, manuals, and established business policies, processes, and procedures, to mention a few. We were learning those and many other things on the fly. In addition, I was the sole investor, and, while our revenue was strong, cash flow was always a challenge. We were hovering somewhere between a mom-and-pop store and a full-fledged corporation. It was a critical time in our growth and development, and we just never could quite get over the hump financially.

The biggest challenge was the seasonality of the business. We would really cook in March, April, and May, then again in July, August, and September. But revenue would drop off considerably during the other six months, and we were unable to generate enough revenue in those slower times to keep the cash flowing throughout the entire year.

I understood that it was a pretty fragile setup. Any big hiccup could knock us on our rear ends, which was what happened in 2004. It was more than a hiccup, though. It was more like an ulcer.

I'll spare you the gory details. Let's just say that I had a disagreement with a supplier that represented 40 percent of our retail sales and 45 percent of our team business. The disagreement led to the supplier closing our account, seemingly overnight. That was the beginning of the end for Soccer Unlimited. A couple of very stressful years later, our bank seized my assets, including all business and personal accounts, to pay debt.

Soccer Unlimited was dead. The $200 cash in my pocket was all the money I had.

It was a very tough time in my life. My heart ached for the employees who had been so loyal, hard-working, and honest over the many years. I felt that I abandoned customers who had been so good to us and vendors who had served us so well. The worst, most unbearable part of it was personal. I had a wife and three children under the age of 12 to care for. Those were the most important people in the world for me to lead, and it was agonizing for me to deal with the notion that I was letting them down.

Remember that stuff I said earlier about how leadership lessons in business can be messy? Well, this was the messiest, most difficult test of leadership I've experienced in my entire life.

When I look back at the wreckage of that moment, it still sends a little bolt of anxiety and nausea through me, even though it was years ago, and I'm doing fine today. Perhaps you who have experienced a similar depth of despair can relate.

And, when I think about the kind of leadership I needed to get through that period of my life, it certainly has its distinctions from my leadership experiences in my family and my soccer journey at IU. But similarities exist, too.

Like my athletic experience. I had to be resilient, had to hang in there, had to get back up and get after it, had to be strong. And, I had to believe in what I was doing. In this case, I had to believe in me.

I also felt that my approach to all my relationships at Soccer Unlimited was very similar to my approach in leading IU's soccer team and similar to the environment my parents created in our home and the communities where we had lived. I'd always tried to be very open and thoughtful of everyone before myself.

All that certainly helped, but one very significant difference existed with the collapse of Soccer Unlimited: my failure at Indiana University wouldn't have affected anyone but me. My situation with Soccer Unlimited affected thousands of people—family, friends, employees, customers, and vendors.

My health was suffering from years of stress, which probably comes as no surprise, and frankly, my marriage was on the rocks. That also should come as no surprise. I saw myself failing the most important responsibility of my life: providing for my family.

Which is why it was extremely—I mean extremely—difficult to find the strength merely to get out of bed on many mornings. I think if I'm being honest with myself, part of what drove me was desperation and panic. I couldn't let down my wife and kids. A former college teammate and roommate, Johnny Johnson, stepped in, wiring money to me from his personal bank account that was enough to get me through one month of expenses. It was as vital as oxygen at that point, and I thank the Good Lord almost every day for JJ's generosity. If he hadn't been there for me, I'm not sure how this crisis would have ended.

That allowed me to focus on the next 30 days and how I would try to rebuild everything—my career, my marriage, and my life. This leadership was different from anything I'd encountered, definitely not the kind you learn about in business school.

After my head cleared, I realized it was up to me, entirely, how I wanted to move forward from what might be considered a devastating setback, a point of no return. People could and did give me advice, and I appreciated that. But ultimately, I decide who I am and, with the Good Lord's guidance, what path I want to walk. I'm not a whiner or a person who feels sorry for himself. Never have been that guy.

I'm a person who learns lessons, bounces back, and moves forward, embracing the next challenge.

I went to work as a commission salesman and committed to doing the best I could every single day. My days as a business owner and entrepreneur were over, but I made a conscious decision that I would work my new job as if I owned the company.

I was grateful for the opportunity my new employer provided, and I owed it to him and to our customers to provide the same level of service and commitment that I'd learned from my Soccer Unlimited days.

We struggled. Sherri and I had our disagreements, shed many tears together, and endured a lot of long, anxious nights.

I knew during this time of struggling to get back on my feet that I wasn't the greatest father I could be. The constant uncertainty and stress of trying to provide financially for my family was all-consuming and kept pounding in my head like a hammer on an anvil. Every single waking minute, I was on edge, and when my head hit the pillow, I couldn't sleep.

We men are hardwired to project invincibility and toughness. As leaders, we should have a measure of that. But one lesson about leadership I learned through this ordeal is that if we embrace that approach too deeply, we actually end up damaging ourselves, our relationships, and often the people we love most.

In this case, those people were Sherri and our three young children. Sherri, of course, grasped what was going on and was as supportive as she could be. But I could see that the children, in particular, were suffering emotionally by all the anxiety in the household, anxiety that emanated from me and created a pressure cooker.

The kids were unable to discern the reasons for my stress, largely because I wanted to project invincibility and pretend that everything was wonderful. It came from a loving place. I didn't want to cause my kids emotional trauma. I wanted to protect them. That's what fathers are supposed to do, right?

It wasn't working. The overall uncertainty of the situation was stressing out our kids much more than necessary. I think the reason is simple. They were confused. They saw that I was very short with them, that I was very distracted and anxious, and that I had closed off a huge part of myself to them. I simply wasn't myself around them. So, like many of us would do, they began to make assumptions and reached what in their minds were logical conclusions: "I must be doing something wrong; something that dad doesn't like." Or, "Dad doesn't like me at all. What did I do to make him not love me anymore? I must be an awful kid."

Thank God I was aware enough to see the potential damage I was inflicting on my children. But I didn't know what to do about it.

Like I said, I didn't want to scare them or make their lives more unsettled. I didn't want them to worry. I wanted to be strong, lead by example, and make them strong. But they saw right through it and started making their own inaccurate conclusions. It was tearing up my insides and pulling our family further apart.

Something in my heart told me to be open with them, to just be who I am and hope for the best. I felt that, as tough as it was for them to go through all this, there was nothing worse than the kids knowing something was wrong but not knowing the cause. You might say I surrendered to the truth, or something much bigger. That something was my faith. In letting go, I was able to find peace and comfort in the journey I was about to face. That time in my life still reminds me of one of my favorite parables, Footprints in the Sand. I'm certain that I was carried through various parts of this journey.

Sherri and I decided to try to explain the situation to them as best as we could, not overburdening them with too many details, but sharing our feelings and thoughts with them throughout, always expressing that things would work out, even if at times it might not have been that evident to me. I was able to assure them that we would all be fine, especially if we stuck together. I told them this was our team. We had to work together as a team, overcome this as a team, and start winning again as a team. I placed a lot of trust in God that honesty and measured transparency was the right decision. It turned out to be the greatest team I ever played for.

The kids responded with an unconditional love that was nothing short of heroic. They were hopeful. They were constantly telling me how much they loved me. They dug into their piggy banks to give me their last dimes. They were the people who I needed the most strength from, and they gave me overflowing amounts. They helped me believe in myself when I needed that the most, and they provided crucial support that I could get nowhere else. They also provided the inspiration and drive I needed to get through this ordeal, along with so many other blessings, through their genuine caring, empathy, and love. I've always been inspired by youth, but never as much as at this particular time in my life.

It also led to the beginning of a tradition I'd had with my family as a kid: gathering around the kitchen table and sharing. When I decided to share my feelings and be transparent with the kids, I did it at the kitchen table, and it was one of the most rewarding "kitchen table" moments of my life. That practice has paved the way for open, honest discussion and an undeniably strong, enduring family bond between Sherri, the kids, and me.

And, this journey provided me with an enduring leadership lesson: In trying to present a false strength, I was isolating myself from Sherri and the kids, causing them more anxiety and confusion. People may perceive my decision to share my thoughts and feelings as weak, but I think the exact opposite now. Hiding myself, closing myself off to them was the fearful, weaker approach that had the potential to inflict great harm on the people I love the most.

It took more courage to share myself with them, to trust their character and a higher power. It was a riskier decision to lay it out there. When I did, I found that human nature is empathetic, supportive, and loving. I was trying to be strong, but until I decided to be transparent with my family, I actually was being weak in terms of true leadership.

It took every ounce of energy we could muster from way down deep. It took a form of leadership that came from our souls. But we hung in there. Underneath it all, everyone had a clear understanding of how deeply I loved them and how much I needed their love—even though we were struggling financially. Maybe because of it. It was a test of my belief in transparency, and it turned out so much healthier for all involved than the invincible approach.

My decision didn't yield perfect results. We're a family like any other. We had our moments. Slowly, Sherri and I rebuilt our relationship and got our feet under us. Now, we have a healthy marriage with a family that is even stronger for having gone through what we did and not given up on each other. Financially, we can see the light at the end of the tunnel.

These circumstances could have blown up the entire family, but today, we're closer than ever and value our time together more than we ever have. We kept the faith and did the hard work that wasn't always pretty, day in and day out, through transparency, trust, and prayer. We never took anything for granted. It was all of us leading each other in maybe the best example of *philotimo* that I can recall in my life. We absorbed invaluable leadership concepts, even if the process of absorbing them was messy and painful.

I also learned a deeper sense of gratitude, another valuable lesson. I'm eternally grateful to so many people: my college buddy, JJ, who came through when I needed it most; my Aunt Georgia, whose incredible generosity helped me repay a chunk of debt; my parents and siblings for literally getting me through the toughest times with their empathy, support, and belief in me; and Sherri and the kids for keeping me inspired, for saying something as simple and seemingly small as "I love you" every night. I realized that most times, true, unconditional love was all I needed to push forward one more day and work as hard as I could.

I'm also grateful for my former customers at Soccer Unlimited who supported me through the entire ordeal and, somehow, never made me feel like a failure. They underscored a leadership and life lesson that you might call karma or energy flow. It's about treating people with kindness and fairness, going the extra mile, establishing those personal relationships. The way I treated people—the strong relationships I created and nurtured over the years—is a consistent theme of my life and helped me in challenging times. If you take a similar approach with others and surround yourself with people who share those life values, you'll get that kind of support and energy in return, not all the time but almost all the time, and it's a wonderful feeling. It makes all that effort worth it. Believe me.

I'm grateful also for the vendors who were willing to work with me, who did their best to keep Soccer Unlimited alive for as long as possible. I live my life every day being grateful for those who have been there for me, and I've made a promise to do the same for them.

And, sometimes, when I'm feeling really encouraged about my prospects, I think about the three things that could have been taken from me—my money, my health, and my family—and I'm grateful I lost the one I could deal with best, my money.

Let me make one other thing very clear: As excruciating as the Soccer Unlimited adventure was at the end, I have never second guessed my decision to join the family business. The strong years were unbelievably rewarding in ways that were much deeper than financial success. In building that company from the ground up, we created some very strong family ties and lifelong relationships and memories with so many people. I needed all of them and their foundations of trust and love to get through the ordeal.

And, you know what? It all worked out very well for me.

As I write this, our family unity is better than it's ever been, I'm coming off one of my most successful years professionally, and my passion to help others through motivational speaking is coming to fruition. I'm a fuller, wiser, more purpose-filled person for having endured what I did and making the decision to be transparent. Most importantly, the value of sitting around the kitchen table has become a saving grace for all of us.

I'm a leader. Maybe not in the conventional sense, but a leader nonetheless.

# CHAPTER 5
# SUPER ALLISON

## LEADERSHIP IN THE COMMUNITY

I've always been a person who enjoys being part of the good that's happening in a community, which is another way of saying that I volunteer a lot. I like to follow my interests and look for chances to volunteer in those areas. It's fun and extremely fulfilling in ways that I think strengthen the soul.

So, I've been a mostly volunteer soccer coach for 30 years and was on the committee that helped position Indianapolis as a potential host city for the 2018 or 2022 World Cup. I've been a volunteer speaker to numerous youth sports organizations and served on the board of a nonprofit that focused on early childhood initiatives. For nearly a decade, I volunteered as a mentor and leader in Peyton's Pals, an arm of Peyton Manning's PeyBack Foundation. I'm chairman of the Bigelow Advisory Board of the Pancreatic Cyst & Cancer Early Detection Center, part of my personal mission to honor a friend who passed away from pancreatic cancer. We'll talk about his remarkable leadership later.

I volunteer on a high school parent resource group. I'm also very involved in my church as a youth minister, among other informal roles. One of my favorites in that informal category came a few years ago when Sherri and I read in the church bulletin that a 92-year-old man moved to the area and needed a ride to church every Sunday. We volunteered, and for two years, we picked up "Pops" from his apartment every single Sunday and took him to church. We introduced him to a lot of people at St. Louis De Montfort, and he became a mainstay in the third pew every Sunday for the 9 a.m. mass. Then, we'd return to his apartment for honey buns, Coke, and some great storytelling. Most times all the kids would come along, too. We still get a chuckle and warm memories recalling our times with "Pops."

Beyond all that, as I mentioned earlier, I've been pretty involved for years in volunteering with Indiana Sports Corp. That's how I met Coach K.

It's also where I met Allison Melangton, who served in a number of leadership roles with the Sports Corp, including president.

One of the many things that impresses me about her is her unassuming openness. Allison knows who she is, and she listens to you, really absorbs what you have to say. She doesn't seem to be afraid of confrontation. In fact, I think she welcomes a difference of opinion. She seems to understand that's how you make real progress, how you build solid, working relationships and sincere collaboration. She is one amazing person who always struck me as kind, deeply spiritual, and extremely humble, someone you could pour out your heart to. She's also petite and soft-spoken, and it always intrigued me that she held all those leadership roles with the Sports Corp and other entities. I was curious about what made her tick and what made her so successful. She is one of those people you just wanted to be around, who have that certain something that makes them special. The more I got to know her, the more I realized what that certain something was.

She just doesn't fit the "type-A" stereotype of leaders. I found that fascinating. That is why I was so inspired one day in 2008 when I picked up the newspaper and saw that she was going to run Indianapolis' first Super Bowl in 2012. I didn't think twice about it. She was a natural fit.

However, if there's one job I might assume would require the most type-A person I could imagine, it would be the CEO and president of the Super Bowl Host Committee. The other assumption would be that person would have been a man.

That's another one of the things I love about Allison. She breaks stereotypes and assumptions and does it without a lot of hoopla.

After the New York Giants beat the New England Patriots 21-17 in the thrilling Super Bowl XLVI, after all the confetti was swept away, and all the visitors returned home, the entire event was widely regarded as the most engaging and successfully organized Super Bowl in history.

Let me give Allison a little hoopla for that. She earned it. And, let me start at the beginning of her story.

Allison was born and raised in Auburn, Maine, a small town about 40 miles north of Portland, and was a gifted gymnast. When it came time for college, she'd received offers from several schools and decided the best place for her would be Colorado State University in Fort Collins, only about 2,100 miles from her home. The choice probably was an early indicator that young Allison was courageous.

She competed as a gymnast for two years at Colorado State, and, when the program was scrapped, Allison shifted to the diving team, which probably suggested that she was not only courageous but also versatile. Allison ended up graduating with a degree in commercial sports management and landing a job with the US Olympic Committee in Colorado Springs.

Then she decided to take a job with USA Gymnastics and move to Indianapolis in the early 1980s. She'd never been to Indiana and knew only one person there—the guy who had traveled to Colorado to interview her for the job.

It was 1983. She needed to find a place to live and a roommate. So, she did what people did back then. She placed an ad in the newspaper looking for a roommate.

"Who does that?" Allison said with a smile one Friday morning in her office at the Indianapolis Motor Speedway, where she is senior vice president of Hulman Motorsports Corporation.

"This girl called me and said, 'I saw your ad in the newspaper. I just graduated from IU,'" Allison recalled, "and we had, like, a four-minute conversation and she said, 'I'll find a place, and I'll mail you a key and tell you when we have it available. I'm like, 'Okay.'"

My, how times have changed.

A few days later, Allison received the letter with a map, a key, the name of the apartment complex, and specific directions on how to get there. She hopped in her car and headed east.

"I remember leaving Colorado, and the Rocky Mountains were in my rearview mirror as I was driving toward Kansas," Allison told me. "I was looking at the mountains through the mirror, and I just started crying. I thought, 'This better work.' I loved Colorado and thought I'd be there forever, but then this opportunity came along. I cried all the way across the state. Then, when I got to the state line, I said, 'Okay, get your big girl pants on. This is the choice you made, and you're going to make the best of it. In two years, if it doesn't work out, you can move back.'"

She arrived at 2 a.m. in the apartment parking lot and sat in her car thinking that the young woman sounded nice and hoping that everything would work out. She walked in the apartment and saw a little welcome note. Her roommate's door was shut. Taped to another door was a piece of paper that read, "Your room." Allison tossed her sleeping bag in the room, closed the door, and slid down her side of it. Then she prayed that this adventure would work.

The two new roommates met the next morning over coffee, and it worked. They lived together for nearly three and a half years until Allison married Tom, who, coincidentally, I went to high school with.

In her job at USA Gymnastics, Allison directed national and international events for 11 years. She also worked at eight Olympic Games, mostly as an associate producer for the gymnastics broadcast by *NBC Sports,* work that earned her five Emmy Awards.

But the gymnastics job kept her on the road all the time, two or three weeks a month, and when she and Tom decided to have a family, Allison wanted to find a position that allowed her to work locally as much as possible. She landed at Sports Corp, where she worked for 20 years, wrapping up her time there as its president before jumping over to Hulman Motorsports in 2014.

It was in about 2006 during her time at Sports Corp that somebody hatched the slightly wild idea of Indianapolis hosting the Super Bowl, specifically, Super Bowl XLVI. The wheels actually had started turning a little earlier. When the Indiana State Legislature passed legislation funding the construction of Lucas Oil Stadium, civic leaders had their eye on the possibility of hosting the big game.

Allison, whose job it was to pull together the city's bids on all sporting events it sought, worked with Fred Glass, president of the city's Capital Improvement Board, and Jack Swarbrick, board chairman of Sports Corp. They went through the NFL's two, three-inch-thick binders of requirements and compiled a bid that I think surprised the NFL, in part because Indianapolis arrived at the bidding meetings with $25 million in funding in hand—the first city to achieve that distinction.

It wasn't enough. Dallas won.

I think in looking at leadership, it's always important to see how a leader deals with serious disappointment and heartbreak, the kind of disappointment that occurs when you work really hard on a huge goal for an extended period and fall short. I asked Allison how much of a disappointment losing the Super Bowl bid was, and her answer provided a small but very telling insight into her life philosophy and her approach to leadership.

"It was a really interesting growing experience for me," she said. She remembered the group of 10 or so traveling to Nashville for two days of meetings, then making the big pitch, and then waiting in a holding room for the voting results. "When Indianapolis Colts owner Jim Irsay and president Bill Polian walked in the room," Allison said, "their expressions showed that they had lost." Irsay shed a few tears saying he felt terrible that he was unable to deliver the game after how hard everyone had worked.

"My heart hurt all of a sudden," Allison said, "but for everybody else in the room. I just started looking around at Jack and Fred and people who really put their lives on hold for us to get this bid. I did, too, but I'm the person who thinks of everybody else before I think of myself. I was just sad for everybody because we had worked so hard, and we thought we deserved to win."

All was not lost. The vote among owners, which reportedly was 17-15 for Dallas, was so close and owners were so impressed with Indy's effort that they strongly suggested the team from Indianapolis return to bid for another Super Bowl.

That seemingly simple task became complicated. Indianapolis mayor, Bart Peterson, a passionate promoter of the Super Bowl in Indianapolis, lost reelection. Then, in 2008, the country went into an economic tailspin.

Fortunately, Peterson's successor, Greg Ballard, also was supportive, but not until after attending a Super Bowl in Phoenix that February. The bid had to be made in May. Mayor Ballard brought in Mark Miles, who had been president of the organizing committee for Indianapolis' hosting of the Pan American Games. Mark, Jack, and Allison put together a second bid, one that had a distinct difference from its predecessor and from all the other bids that year. This bid proposed an unprecedented level of community development. The idea was to make the Super Bowl about lasting change in Indianapolis and beyond, change that would be more than the one-time economic infusion that all Super Bowls provide the host city. This kind of change would focus on community development in the context of engaging the community in the game in ways that connected people and improved lives for years to come.

It worked. NFL owners chose Indianapolis. It was the city's first Super Bowl.

"This time when they came in and told us we won, I started crying," Allison said. "The first time, when we lost, I didn't. We were kind of sad and like, 'Wow, I can't believe we didn't win it.' The second time, it was like a release of energy."

That was in May of 2008. Reality set in quickly. Jack or Fred probably was the logical, conventional choice to lead the organizing effort, Allison thought. Then Jack left to take the University of Notre Dame athletic director job in July 2008, and Fred was close behind, leaving in January of 2009 to take the Indiana University athletic director job.

Right around that time, Allison got a phone call from Mark Miles. He and Mayor Ballard wanted her to be CEO and president of the Super Bowl.

"We had a really good family discussion on it that night," Allison recalled. "My son [Cameron] was a freshman in high school. I knew taking that job meant that all of us were taking the job, and it was going to be a full-press, four-year commitment."

She was very upfront about the magnitude of the commitment. The three of them talked about the reality that Allison would miss some of Cameron's soccer games. She and Tom, who is co-owner of a heating and cooling company, had split chores and related responsibilities at home. She knew taking the job would place 90 percent of that on him.

"And, if that's not how we can do it," she recalled telling them, "then I'm not going to take the job, because you guys are my most important priority."

She said the sacrifice Tom and Cameron would have to make was the toughest part in deciding whether to take the job. Even after the two of them bought in, Allison was unsure. In the end, the decision came down to the position being a once-in-a-lifetime opportunity and them knowing she was the best person for the job. Most important of all perhaps was that the job had a finite length.

"I would have never taken it if this was going to be my life," Allison said. "This was going to be four years, and then we'd go back to what life balance is."

And that's how Allison Melangton became the big cheese of Super Bowl XLVI, only the second woman to head a Super Bowl. Here's an interesting detail: Since Allison took the position, women have filled the role in three Super Bowls.

While Mayor Ballard and Mark Miles had confidence in Allison's ability to do the job—she'd proven herself time and time again—others in the community might have been less confident. That became clear one morning after the official announcement was made that she was president. Allison stopped at an auto repair shop to get the oil changed on her Saab.

The shop had a shuttle to take customers to their workplaces while their cars were out of commission. Allison jumped in the back of the van. Four men stepped in front, followed by the driver, who flipped on the radio. A Super Bowl commercial came on the air.

"When it ended," Allison told me, "this guy right in front of me says, 'Can you believe our city hired a woman to run the Super Bowl? I don't know what Mayor Ballard was thinking.' And, he goes on and on and on."

She could feel her neck getting a little warm. Then it got a little warmer.

"I'm just sitting there thinking, 'Okay,' and the conversation goes on," Allison said. "No personal attacks, but the conversation was about the audacity of thinking that a woman could run our Super Bowl and how embarrassing it was going to be when it failed."

Her temperature rising, Allison thought about her options for an appropriate response. She said she could remember vividly that feeling and the conversation like it was yesterday, like it was burned in her brain, even though it happened nearly a decade ago.

Sitting there in the van, her anger percolating, she figured she had three choices.

"My first choice is to say something," Allison recalled. "Then, probably what comes out is not reflective of the person I am."

I had to chuckle and marvel at her introspection.

"B, I can get out of the car and then hand them all a business card and tell them that I hope they're proud of what we'd accomplished in the end."

That seemed appropriate.

"Or C, I could get out and say absolutely nothing and then hope that, in the end, they will have a different opinion in two years."

From my perspective, that would have been the toughest option.

"I remember saying to myself, 'Well, what would Jesus do?' And then"—she snapped her fingers—"that was it. I knew exactly what I'd do."

She stepped out of the van and said nothing.

"That was the right thing to do for me," Allison told me. "Not for everyone else, but it was the right thing to do for me."

That episode was an indication of what was ahead of her.

A few weeks later, Allison hired a woman with the ideal experience to help organize a Super Bowl. She'd worked and lived in the Washington, DC area for about 20 years, serving for a time as Dick Cheney's political director. Of more relevance was that she'd run a Republican national convention. I didn't know this until Allison informed me, but the Republican and Democratic national conventions are the only events that require more logistical and security know-how than a Super Bowl.

The woman grew up in South Bend and had graduated from Indiana University. She was looking to return to Indiana to be closer to her father after her mother had passed away.

"So, I got her, and she was perfect because she had all this incredible security and operational experience and everything else," Allison told me.

She'd been on the job maybe two months when she stepped in Allison's office at the end of a work day and asked to talk. She shut the door behind her.

"I know we don't know each other very well," Allison recalled her saying, "but I'm really ticked off at you."

Okay, Allison said. How come?

"I think you're running the whole thing wrong," she told Allison. "I've been watching for two months. You've got this all wrong."

Okay, Allison said. What's wrong about it?

"We're never going to get anything done because you're too nice to everybody," she said. "All you want to do is put partners together, and you want to work together. When there's a problem, you get everybody in the same room. You're just collaborating all the time. The Super Bowl's in, like, three years. It's not in 10 years. It's in three years. We are never going to get there with that approach."

On and on she went, saying that in Washington, DC, they operate in an entirely different, more forceful, decisive way. She said how much Allison frustrated her. Throughout the woman's venting, Allison sat there taking it all in, repeating, "Okay, okay."

Finally, when the woman finished, Allison told her she really wanted the relationship to work.

"I want you to tell me these things," Allison told her. "But we're going to do it my way, and my way is we are going to partner with these people. When we have a problem with the parking lot operators, and we have a problem with the stadium, we're going to get everyone in a room. We're not going to tell them what to do. We are going to work with them to come up with solutions together, and then we're going to get those solutions and put them into action. But, I'm not going to run around, and we're not going to tell everybody in Indianapolis that this is how we're doing it because that's not what's happening."

"She said, 'Then we're never going to get it done.' I said, 'We're going to get it done. I promise.'"

The truth was that Allison was more than overwhelmed with the job. She described the first six months as chaos. It felt to her as if everyone in the state had an idea or product or some other pitch they wanted to make to her or wanted to volunteer. From almost day one, she and her very lean staff of two were receiving 400 voicemail messages a day—so many that voicemail kept shutting down. She recalled one day getting 1,000 emails.

It was the same routine every day. She'd get up at 5 a.m., rush to work, and be hit with a tsunami. She'd get home really late, exhausted, crawl into bed, and start it all over again the next morning. She felt like a hamster in a wheel, except unlike the hamster, Allison knew she wasn't staying in the same place. She was losing ground and feeling very discouraged.

"I finally understood what drinking out of the fire hose was," she told me, "but it was like the nozzle was in my mouth."

At church one Sunday, a close friend, Denise Howell, asked how she was doing. Allison said she was trying to keep her head above water. The friend forced Allison to go to coffee, even though Allison said she was too busy.

When the two started talking, Allison spilled everything to her about feeling overwhelmed with the job and missing her son's soccer games and not being there for friends when they needed her. Everything was so out of balance, and it felt like nothing was getting done. She was really frustrated.

Her friend thought what Allison was experiencing was a spiritual imbalance, that she'd lost touch with perhaps the most important component of who she was: her faith. The words rang like a bell in Allison's mind.

The friend reached in her purse and gave Allison an index card and a rubber band. Then she gave her simple instructions: Every Sunday, she wanted Allison to write down what she was praying for on one side of the card. On the other, she directed Allison to write a question: What did I do to honor God today? She told Allison to use the rubber band to place it on the visor in her car. For the next 30 days, she asked Allison to concentrate on one side of the card during her drive to work and the other side of the card on her way home.

"I did that, and it totally changed my life," Allison told me. For her 30-minute morning commute, she prayed for her son Cameron, husband Tom, and others who needed prayer. When she reached the office, she found that she was calm and focused, that her heart and mind were in the right place for the start of the day. She had the ideal perspective to lead her employees.

"In the morning, I didn't let my mind go crazy on the way to work and have it be all chaotic and cluttered when I got there."

On the commute home, Allison turned to the other side of the card, reviewing what she did to honor God that day. It reminded and reinforced her values and how she walks through life.

"It was really cleansing for me because I was forced to do it in the car," Allison recalled, "and it was the perfect time in my life to go into that discipline."

It was fascinating to me. I asked what happened to the hundreds of contacts every day, the demands on her time that were pulling her in three or four or five directions at any given moment.

Those hadn't changed, Allison said, but for some reason they weren't eating her up inside. She processed and managed them differently. You might call it the mystery of faith.

"I was refocused on what defines me, and what defines me is my faith and my family and my relationships with people I care about," she told me. "That discipline helped me get the focus back that wasn't just, 'I'm the Super Bowl; everything in my life is the Super Bowl.' It sort of brought me back to the understanding that I know who I am in God's eyes, and in my eyes and I know I'm going to tackle this, and we're going to get through it and do it. We dug in and got organized instead of being paralyzed."

I found it really interesting that she had been experiencing very little fulfillment of who she was by what she was doing, even though so many people would approach her and tell her that president of the Super Bowl must be the best thing in her life. And the more she heard that, the more she came to realize that was untrue.

It was a great opportunity, and she was extremely grateful to have it, but it wasn't who she was. It was what she was doing. I think she was paralyzed by letting all the chaos overtake that sense of who she really was. Once she galvanized in her mind what is at her core, she found true purpose in how to do her job.

"I'll tell you, after that, there was never a day that I felt overwhelmed or exhausted, even though I was those things and was as busy as I've ever been. I'd hit reset and was re-grounded in who I was. I never got sick in four years. And, it was interesting because a lot of people kept coming to me after I had sort of worked through that myself and would say I was so calm."

I think a lot of what we accomplish comes down to why we accomplish it, if that makes any sense. Sometimes discipline, if it's the right discipline, helps liberate us to see that why.

Once she found the why, Allison also revived the heart—some might say the *philotimo*—of her leadership philosophy. It manifested itself in the collaborative, personal approach she took to the job.

Hers was almost the polar opposite of the NFL's heavy-handed history in dealing with host communities, but she managed to navigate that and stay focused on what she and Mark Miles, who was board chairman of the host committee, had set as the goal of this Super Bowl: making it, and all that was happening around it and leading up to it, the most inclusive Super Bowl in history.

Just as they'd noted in their pitch to NFL owners in May, the two of them continued to follow through on their vision that the Super Bowl was much more than an economic opportunity. They had talked early and often about this event, providing a rare moment to pull the entire state together for more than a few days or a week before the event. Allison knew the best way to accomplish that was to use a collaborative approach.

"We're going to love people through these relationships, and we're not going to be the big, heavy foot that comes in and then stomps on everybody," Allison told me when I asked her to elaborate on her approach to hosting the big game. "We weren't going to be shoving this Super Bowl down everybody's throat. We were going to find ways for people to enjoy and engage in doing it. More than anyone else, our community's going to benefit from hosting this game."

It was related to what she told me about what the top priority of a leader should be: getting the most out of your people, inspiring them to be the best they can be while working together as a team. That's the only way you achieve a high-performing team, she said. If they are high individual achievers but not working together, you're not going to get anything done.

And, if you are hammering the team members all the time, you isolate and limit people—a lesson she absorbed from her years in team sports, she said. That relentless, agitated approach inspires little more than resentment, contempt, and misery. Many people in her field of sports management come from team athletics. So, she's seen how they—and everyone else—respond to collaborative, inspiring leadership that you might find in a truly great coach.

"Just screaming and yelling at them all the time and demanding that they run faster doesn't work," Allison said.

I asked how she established that culture working with an organization like the NFL and even some of her own people who believed in a more, shall we say, assertive approach.

Transparency and trust, Allison said.

"The central part of all of that is trust," she added. "You have to make them trust you, and you trust them, and they have to trust each other. It's this little trust circle and that only comes from hard work, honesty, daily contact, and communication…and cultivating it."

Allison did that by talking a lot every day to a lot of people. She'd studied host committees of previous Super Bowl cities, which didn't emphasize that intense community conversation, and saw that those communities hadn't responded in the way she was hoping for Indianapolis.

Her fundamental message sent throughout the Super Bowl organizing group was that people working for her were going to talk with everybody who reached out to them, no matter how angry or excited, how focused or scatterbrained, whether they had an idea or just wanted to help. And, if one of her staff didn't want to talk with a particular person, Allison would. The strategy built what she called "a groundswell of support for us," a trust throughout the community.

"There aren't many opportunities in any city to get everybody on the same page, with all the social issues that go on in the world, the varying views and opinions," she said. "Our whole project, everything we did, was with the view that this is more than a game. It's not about what actually happens on the field, even though most of the world thinks that's what it's about. For us, it's about building community, changing peoples' lives, positive impact, great moments, making people feel valued. So, all the projects we did we said, 'This has to positively impact the city, or we're not going to do it.'"

Her crew embraced the excitement that was everywhere around the city and state. Then they channeled it in a bunch of different directions, a little like a Fourth of July firework that soars in the sky, bursts in one core of light, and fans out. All those calls and emails that overwhelmed her at the outset now were being formed into an organized volunteer force of 8,000 spread throughout the community and beyond.

Allison set up 62 leadership committees, about four times more than the number for any previous Super Bowl, and placed 160 leaders in charge of those committees. Those leaders committed to working in the community for three years. She used the entire network in part to engage and train the next generation of civic and community leaders by partnering a seasoned veteran in one area—transportation, for example—with a young person.

"We told them, 'This matters to us, and we don't care, as a young leader, if you don't engage in sports anymore,'" Allison said, "'but we want you to engage in something. We want you to be civically engaged.'"

The committee created new initiatives and augmented others. People throughout the community responded.

One of the most tangible ways was the Near Eastside Legacy Project, an effort started a few years earlier to revitalize a largely forlorn neighborhood steps from Indianapolis' thriving downtown. In fact, the city's team that bid for the Super Bowl cited the legacy project as one of its primary mechanisms to use the game for community enhancement.

Once the NFL chose Indianapolis, the project gained powerful momentum. Through the Super Bowl Legacy Initiative, nearly $154 million in federal, state, local, business, foundational, and private investment was made in the Near Eastside. That included money for housing upgrades such as new, affordable housing and the rehabilitation of more than 30 vacant and abandoned homes. Funds also were used to build the $11 million Chase Near Eastside Legacy Center, a multipurpose facility that, among other services, provides wellness and fitness programs.

In addition to those bricks and mortar efforts, other powerful initiatives sprung up.

While watching football highlights with a close friend battling breast cancer, Allison noticed pink gear on the players, and pink t-shirts, caps, and jackets fans wore throughout the stadiums—all part of the

NFL's campaign to raise breast cancer awareness. An idea popped in her mind.

She thought of the Susan G. Komen for the Cure Tissue Bank at the Indiana University Simon Cancer Center, which collects blood samples, breast tissue, and saliva for researchers all over the world. In July 2011, Allison and her staff announced Super Cure, which included hosting tissue donation events and fundraisers for the tissue bank. She persuaded pro-basketball star Tamika Catchings and Emmy-Award-winning Indianapolis anchorwoman Anne Marie Tiernon, among others, to donate tissue.

"Women aren't typically a segment that is involved in the Super Bowl," Allison told me, "but we wanted to get them involved and we thought, 'How are we going to do that?'"

One million dollars was raised for the bank, and, during Indy's Super Cure weekend, 700 healthy breast tissue donations were collected.

A year earlier, in early 2010, the Host Committee began working on a variety of green initiatives to counter the Super Bowl's carbon footprint, an effort that led to more than 1 million pounds of carbon and 2.5 million gallons of water conserved.

A staggering 200,000 students across Indiana participated in community programs through the Super Bowl. That number included nearly 200 high school students who were a huge part of a campaign that set a goal of planting 2,012 trees to align with the 2012 Super Bowl. Residents blew by that number and planted nearly 3,000 trees. In addition, a total of 43,000 pounds—that's 21 tons—of unwanted electronics that otherwise would have gone to landfills were collected for recycling.

About 1,000 volunteers packed 7,000 Super Baskets of Hope, which were sent to critically ill children in hospitals in 32 NFL cities. Folks collected gently used and new sporting goods, books, and school supplies for distribution to children in need. Groups even figured out ways to recover 46,000 pounds of food from Super Bowl events and distribute them to those in need.

Then there was involvement from the arts. A committee of about a dozen artists, museum staffers, architects, cultural advocates, and university representatives administered an effort called "46 for XLVI," a wide assortment of 46 large, vivid murals in public areas. Many were within walking distance of Lucas Oil Stadium, site of the game, or in the Near Eastside neighborhood.

But the quirkiest and perhaps most popular of all these initiatives was Super Scarves, which Allison and her friend Connie Israel came up with about two years into her run as president and CEO of the host committee.

She was at home one night chatting with Connie about hundreds and hundreds of phone calls from older people who, in the rich tradition of Indiana residents, wanted to help with the effort. But she had nothing for them.

"Most of the stuff I had were computer things, and these people who were calling me weren't able to fill Excel spreadsheets or set things up physically. So, I had a population of people who were dying to help me but who I couldn't engage. And, most of them were women. I had this amazing energy with these people, and I wasn't going to be the buzzkill that doesn't get them involved."

The two friends got out a white board and started brainstorming.

"What all these people wanted to do was give to someone else," Allison recalled of the phone callers, "and the volunteers we already had wanted to feel appreciated."

Why not have the elderly folks knit scarves for the Super Bowl volunteers, Allison and Connie thought. It was an idea they'd heard about in the 2008 Special Olympics. Leading up to those games, volunteers made scarves for all of the participants. Allison and Connie thought a similar effort would satisfy all the older people who have time and make the volunteers feel appreciated.

She called Mark Miles the next day.

"He said, 'Scarves, knitting, and Super Bowl don't go in the same sentence. You can't do it,'" Allison recalled. "I said, 'Hear me out. This is going to engage people. This is going to make people feel valued. We're going to connect people because each of these scarves is going to have a handwritten note from the person who did it. They're going to tell them why they knitted it, why they wanted to help the volunteers. So, the person who gets it will feel special when they get it. We're going to ask people across the state to do it, and this is going to connect our people all over the state.'"

Mark's response: "The NFL is going to think you're crazy. We're not going to come out and say one of our key programs is knitting scarves. We're not doing it."

Allison persisted, asking how she could convince him. Mark told her to call Ann Murtlow, who was his board chairman at Central Indiana Corporate Partnership, and whose opinion he apparently trusted. If Ann liked the idea, Mark told Allison, he'd give the green light to the scarves campaign. Well, Ann happened to be a knitter. She thought the idea was terrific.

Allison was off to the races. Mark, for all his early opposition, made her feel empowered now.

"Okay," Allison recalled Mark telling her, "but if you're going to do this, we're going to have a big, bold scarf program."

Local libraries offered classes in knitting, crocheting, and weaving. It turned out all those interested weren't only grannies in Kokomo—not that there's anything wrong with them. Allison's scarf committee partnered with women inmates at a state prison who sewed Super Bowl patches on each of the scarves. When the *Indianapolis Star* published a story about the partnership, Allison got a call from the men's warden at the prison.

It turns out male inmates had heard about the partnership and were upset that they weren't involved. Think about it, the warden reminded Allison. A lot of these guys will be released soon, and they are very unhappy with you.

He had Allison's attention. They talked, and she offered to send a volunteer to the prison to teach the inmates to knit. Nearly 20 guys took classes and sent scarves. Later, when they were released, the men met regularly—the same time they had their knitting class every week—to perform community service together.

Other individual scarf stories Allison shared with me were heartwarming, like Bev Meska's. She was an 82-year-old great-grandmother from Michigan City, Indiana, who ended up making more than 250 scarves. Other scarf makers created theirs at hospital bedsides; one woman made hers while she was undergoing kidney dialysis.

Each one had a personal note from the maker, and Allison regularly would see volunteers who received the scarves weep after reading the notes.

She showed me pictures of the scarves—all custom-made—featuring the blue and white colors of the Indianapolis Colts. Some were very basic designs. Others were incredibly elaborate and stylish.

"In the end, we had 13,000 people knit scarves, and they came from all over the globe," Allison told me. "We had Hoosiers in Africa and all these places who were knitting scarves and mailing them to us with these amazing notes, saying, 'I finally feel connected to something going on in Indiana. I've lived in Africa for two years, and now I feel that I can at least be there and contribute to be part of the Super Bowl.'"

I later found the specific breakdown. People in 45 states, Washington, DC, and four countries beyond the US—England, Canada, South Africa, and Belgium—made a total of 13,026 scarves. Not bad considering the goal was 8,000. Allison still sees people wearing them, including a certain, one-time skeptic, Mark Miles.

"Oh my gosh," Allison said, "he's told me a hundred times he is so sorry."

Overall, the Super Bowl XLVI leadership journey was quite a ride for Allison, one that she said was a remarkable learning experience. I asked her for specifics on what in her career, including Super Bowl XLVI, were formative in her becoming a leader.

She said she was grateful for amazing mentors, including Jack Swarbrick and Mark Miles, and that every effective leader has to have those top-quality mentors. The mentorship she received from Jack and Mark has inspired her to create great leaders in younger people.

When I asked what made them model examples, she said Mark's transparency ("he doesn't have a guard") taught her the value of being transparent. That open relationship between her and her employees is critical, she said.

Jack, she added, is an amazing visionary who can look down the road 10 years and paint a picture.

"One of the traits of a good mentor is that they're going to be honest with you when they need to tell you something," she said. "They're going to love you but not sugarcoat it."

Jack had that gift, too, which he displayed for Allison when the two of them—great friends and close business colleagues—were flying to the Olympics in Atlanta, Georgia, for a presentation. It was 6 in the morning, and Allison was talking about the presentation, and talking about the presentation, and talking about the presentation. Finally, Jack reached over and grabbed her hand.

"I love you," Allison recalled him saying, "but I'm going to tell you something. You need to learn to be comfortable in silence."

*Ouch.*

"And, he was right," Allison said. "That was a good lesson for me, but I knew he loved me enough to tell me that. That was 1996. It's a lesson that I listened to and use a lot. You don't need to fill the air when no one's saying anything. And, as a leader, that's not even a good tactic. You've got to let your people talk. But, when I was in quiet situations and no one was talking, I felt like someone should talk, so then, I did."

Mark Miles and Sandy Knapp, former executive director of the Sports Corp, have been similarly honest with her over the years, Allison said, always with the goal of making her better, not to demean her. Allison trusted that was their primary motive.

"Trust is the core of people following a leader," she said when we were wrapping up. "It's hard to follow someone when you don't trust them. And, trust takes time to build. Without it, you can't lead. I think that's true in any industry. You don't want to buy things from people you don't trust. You don't want to follow up on things from people you don't trust. You don't want to work for someone you don't trust.

"So, even if leaders have quirks or habits or whatever the things are that can make them not an exceptional leader, if you don't have trust, you're not going to go anywhere."

I asked Allison about the future of leadership.

She said people feel more disconnected, partly because of technology. It's an intriguing contradiction that I'm hearing more and more. Technology, for all its amazing capacity to connect us electronically, has led to less and less human contact. We are now less inclined to sit across the table from each other and interact.

"How people think about collaborating is changing," Allison said. "People isolate more than they used to, and there are lots of reasons for that. So, I think leaders now have to aggressively engage people in ways that make them comfortable to start and mold them to try to work better in teams."

Are you a pleaser? I asked.

"I don't know if I'm a pleaser," Allison said. "I'm a lover. I love people and want people to enjoy their work environment, enjoy each other, enjoy their projects, and, when they don't, I want to figure it out. If they're not loving what they're doing and they're not passionate about their thing, I'll move people because you're never going to get their full commitment, their full excitement, their full abilities unless they're loving what they're doing.

"I want to be passionate about solving problems."

One other thing popped into my head before I left. I wanted to hear what happened with the woman who stepped in Allison's office and told her how frustrating and aggravating it was to watch Allison's leadership style and that it could lead to a Super Bowl failure.

As it turned out, the staffer was an all-star, Allison said, and jumped on board with the collaborative approach and followed Allison's lead.

"She wrote me the most amazing card after the Super Bowl," Allison said. "She said—and I'll never forget the opening line—'You softened me when I didn't even know I had to be softened. Washington had turned me into someone who forgot how to really talk to people, really listen, really collaborate, and enjoy people. I'm so thankful that I'm now back to the person I was meant to be.'"

# CHAPTER 6
# HE IS HERE IN SO MANY WAYS

## LEADERSHIP IN FRIENDSHIP

When our oldest child, Katrina, was five, I'd heard about a recreational soccer league in our town and figured it was the perfect way for her to start playing the game. Nothing too serious, just an informal platform to learn about the sport and teamwork, stay active, and, most important, have fun. I volunteered to coach Katrina's team.

A few days later, I got a phone call from another dad who I'd bumped into at the kindergarten ice cream social and seen around the neighborhood. Like Katrina, his daughter Kate was five years old. The two girls were in the same kindergarten class. He'd heard that I had played college soccer and, figuring that qualified me as an expert, wanted Kate on my team.

That was cool, but selecting players to teams was a pretty random exercise. Something like 2,000 kids had registered in this league. I told him the only way to assure that Kate would be on my team was if he coached with me. That's exactly what he wanted to do, he said, but he warned me upfront that he knew nothing about soccer.

That was how I got to know Mike Bigelow, the guy who would become perhaps my closest friend and mentor. Over the next nine years, he gave me the most meaningful and powerful leadership lesson of my life. Gave it to countless others, too.

Our collaborative intentions got off to a rocky start, though, and it was basically my fault.

Over the phone, I told him it would be great to have help. Don't sweat the fact that you don't know soccer, I said. It's a fairly simple game, and, remember, we're coaching five-year-old girls. I told him just to show up at the first practice, and I'd get him up to speed. Before you realize it, everything will be rolling along smoothly, I said. I set our first practice for a Monday afternoon.

Then I bailed on him.

Not on purpose. I got stuck at an office an hour and a half away from the practice field, and called to tell him.

"I hate to do this to you, Mike, but I can't make practice," I said. "You'll have to run things on your own this first time."

He really let me have it, asking how in the world could I do that to the kids and how could I expect him to run a practice for these 15 or so easily distracted, largely clueless little girls when he knew absolutely nothing about the game. And, by the way, he said, how is this going to look to the dozen or so parents who were expecting a crisp start to their daughters' soccer experience? He knew how, and he told me in very specific, slightly graphic terms that he'd be the one that parents would associate with this misstep.

I remember apologizing a lot.

As bad as I felt for letting Mike down, I knew one thing for sure:

Those girls were going to have a blast that afternoon. In the short time that I'd gotten to know him a little better, I could see that Mike was a guy who loved life and loved kids, all kids. Those girls might not learn much about soccer at their first practice, but they were going to enjoy the experience of their first day with Coach Mike. And that would be the absolute ideal situation because at that young age, it's all about making the experience so much fun that the kids want to come back and keep playing.

I don't know what Mike did to prepare that afternoon. My guess is he went online and combed through hundreds of drills and ideas and came up with a plan. Whatever he did, it all went well, better than well. At the next practice, all the girls showed up excited to play. To be honest, Mike was so dialed in at that second practice, I'm not sure he even needed me then or for the rest of that season. He obviously had picked up the game quickly, which made me realize another element to his personality. Mike Bigelow is an extremely bright guy.

We ended up making a great coaching team. I had some soccer knowledge. He had an authentic passion for the kids and enthusiasm and optimism that spread throughout the team. We practiced twice a week and played games on Saturdays.

We also became fast friends. I started calling him Bigs. Like me, he was a passionate Chicago Cubs fan and loved to play golf. He also followed the Indianapolis Colts closely. We each had two daughters the same ages, and our sons were only a couple years apart. His favorite movie was *It's a Wonderful Life*, which happens to be one of my favorites as well.

I learned that he was born in Tampa, spent much of his childhood living in the northwest Chicago suburb of Buffalo Grove, and decided at age 10 that he wanted to be an attorney. His family moved to Carmel,

Indiana, in 1982. He enrolled as a sophomore at Cathedral High School, where he started dating a girl named Kris Kennelly, played on the school tennis team, was elected student council president, and graduated with honors.

Bigs went on to the University of Dayton where he majored in history and graduated summa cum laude. Then he enrolled at Vanderbilt Law School, one of the nation's top 20 law schools, and became an editor of the *Law Review*. He passed the Indiana Bar Exam while still in his final year at Vanderbilt, and, after working for about five years at a prominent Indianapolis law firm, Bigs moved to Eli Lilly, the pharmaceutical giant based in Indianapolis.

Eight years after he and Kris had their first date, they got married. He worked his way to assistant general counsel at Lilly, which meant Bigs was in line to become the company's next general counsel. He said he loved the mix of law and business that his job provided.

So, here was this very smart, handsome, highly accomplished guy married to his lovely high school sweetheart with three cute little kids, living in a very desirable neighborhood outside Indianapolis. A guy who had every reason to walk around puffy-chested.

Except that wasn't him. For all his exuberance, Bigs was one of the most unassuming guys I knew. Nothing flashy or fancy about him. He always made it about everyone else.

"Mike never wanted to be the center of attention," Kris told me one afternoon, "but he always was. People were just drawn to him."

Precisely why so many people were drawn to Bigs I think comes down to one thing: presence. He had a gift for being fully engaged in the moment with whoever it was he was hanging with, and he mixed that with empathy, intense enthusiasm, humor, and a knowledge base that was mind blowing. He was a voracious reader, especially fond of history, and knew about everything—sports, rock 'n roll, movies, history, the law, and religion. And, he loved people, loved being surrounded by people.

We enjoyed our coaching experiences so much that we ended up setting aside one Thursday night a month and meeting at Fionn MacCool's, a welcoming, Irish-themed place in Fishers, Indiana, where Bigs and I lived. He was an Irish-American who loved his Guinness and Smithwick's.

Those nights were little gems on my calendar. Just he and I sitting around talking, having a beer or two. No distractions. One of the best things about being around Bigs in those situations was that he always took the conversation to deeper, more meaningful places. We might start off talking about the Cubs or the Colts or some sporting event or the weather or local news, but he'd direct the conversation elsewhere, often about what was going on in my life.

If, for example, I had mentioned an upcoming sales call, Bigs would remember and ask me about it the next time we were together. Then he'd inject some advice or other thoughts, looking to help, always encouraging. I remember when I was struggling with Soccer Unlimited, he was always there to listen, digest what I was telling him, and offer insight.

Over time, Mike expanded the Thursday night Fionn MacCool group to guys who fit well with our penchant for fun and introspection. The two of us grew to six: Mike Melloh, a vice president of human resources; Mike Meskis, a pilot; Marshall Trusler, an orthopedic surgeon; and Mark Wright, a prominent attorney in Indy. We'd all block out that one Thursday night a month for Fionn's. We had a lot of laughs and talked a lot, of course, again with Bigs always taking the conversations to deeper, unpredictable places, always so engaged and engaging. When it was time to wrap up, he would give each of us a hug and say, "I love you." On those few nights where we'd finish without resolving a debate—whether it swirled around who Fionn MacCool was or the lyrics to a song—all of us would wake up the next morning to find an email from Bigs waiting for us. He had researched the topic and provided the correct answer. Almost always, that correct answer reflected the position he took the night before.

Bigs just knew how to connect with people. His listening focus was phenomenal and non-judgmental. His conversational timing was impeccable. He spoke precisely with deep wisdom, compassion, and empathy. I wondered where he got that presence—you might call it mindful engagement—and asked Kris once.

They were seniors in high school when two classmates at Cathedral died—one in a car crash, the other after fighting cancer. Those deaths struck something deep in Bigs, Kris said. He seemed to open up more to her and to others, to draw everyone in his life closer to him. It was as if those two deaths made Bigs realize how fragile and precious our relationships are and that there is no reason to take them for granted or, in a broader context, fail to embrace every moment of life. It was a pretty insightful conclusion for a teenager to take from the heartbreak, shock, and confusion of those deaths. Many kids—and adults—might use them as another reason to become callous and removed, cynical and bitter. They might interpret those deaths as another confirmation that life is unfair and randomly cruel.

Bigs decided to walk in the exact opposite direction and didn't look back.

So, his demeanor may have been learned, or he may have been born with it. More than likely, it was a combination of both. I'm not sure it matters. I'm just grateful that the guy who started out as my assistant coach for a little girls' soccer team was next to me to show me the path.

The two of us coached Kate and Katrina for about five years. We won some games, and we lost some, but the constant was that we— the entire team—had a boatload of fun throughout our run. It was wonderful to grow as fathers and coaches while we watched our two daughters grow up together.

When Kate got to be 10 years old, she moved on to the more competitive travel league. Katrina decided to stay with the rec league, which was fine. I continued coaching her. I kept coaching with Bigs, too.

It turns out that our second daughters—his Maggie and my Nicolette— also were interested in soccer. So, Bigs and I teamed up again. Between both sets of daughters, we were coaching partners for about a decade, which meant we got to know each other about as well as two guys can. I learned an enormous amount from him, about coaching, being a father, husband, and friend.

As a leader and mentor, he definitely would push me further than I believed I could go. I can cite any number of times where he challenged me to be better, always believing in me. Sometimes those challenges could be blunt and forceful, another great leadership trait.

Like the time at MacCool's when I'd shared the latest chapter in my saga in the soccer retail business. It must have been the third or fourth consecutive time that I'd brought it up during our Thursday night gatherings. Bigs sighed and then seized the moment.

"I'm so sick of listening to you whine," he told me at the start of a diatribe that went for about five minutes. "Wake up, man, and get some fire in your belly. Right now, you don't have it. Decide what you're going to do and get after it. You have to own this."

When he finished, nobody said a word. We all knew he'd nailed it with power and precision, like stroking a beautiful line drive off the tee deep down the middle of the fairway.

It stung, but it also rang true. Every word. And, I needed to hear it at that particular moment. After, he put his arm around my shoulder, gave me a hug, and told me I could do it, that it would all be fine, and we moved on.

I did get the fire in my belly and take ownership. It was tough, really tough, but he was right. Once I got after it, everything turned out fine, better than fine.

He played that role with many people in his life, including his younger brother, Brian. To help inspire Brian as he faced the challenges of his freshman year at the University of Dayton, Bigs wrote his younger brother a letter giving him constructive advice. The upshot was that someone out there will always be better than you at something, and that's okay. What's not okay, his older brother wrote, is to let someone beat you at something simply because they outworked you.

"I think the quote was, 'Don't ever let someone beat you at something simply because they worked harder than you did,'" Brian told me. "'You can't help it if someone has more natural talent than you do, but you can control how much effort you put into something.'"

Bigs also included a paraphrase of one of his favorite Mark Twain quotes to help Brian avoid procrastination: "If you have to eat a frog, don't stare too long," Bigs wrote. "If you have to eat two frogs, it's best to eat the bigger one first."

In the envelope Bigs placed a keychain with the famous Nike slogan, "Just Do It."

Today Dr. Brian Bigelow is a highly regarded cardiologist.

Bigs would push the girls, too, but in ways that were optimistic, constructive, and affirmative, never negative, manipulative, or demeaning. He got the most and the best out of the players and me in ways that would maximize the performance of the team as a whole. It was always about the team with Bigs. In all my experience with the game, I've never seen anything quite like his approach.

Everyone responded the same way to Bigs, except maybe coaches of the teams we competed against.

It might come as no surprise that he was a very competitive guy; at times, maybe too competitive. Bigs hated to lose at anything. In fact, he may have hated losing more than he liked winning.

That intense competitive streak could create a little friction between us, particularly when our teams were up by 6 or 7 or more goals, and I'd suggest pulling back our players, ratcheting the level of intensity down a few notches. Not Bigs. He would have none of it. Right there on the sidelines, we'd get into some pretty animated discussions about what I believed was good sportsmanship and what he believed were valuable life lessons about never taking your foot off the gas and never taking anything for granted.

Opposing coaches whose teams were getting pummeled by us shared my view, and that could make for some awkward, post-game moments. But, we got through it.

He had ambitious personal and professional goals, but those never came at the cost of his highest priority, his family. He loved coaching his kids and was famous for planning all the details of adventurous family vacations. One of his often-repeated quotes to his kids was, "You can never have too many friends."

Another one that often pops into my head and brings a smile is from the brilliantly witty writer Oscar Wilde: "Everything in moderation, including moderation," which I always took as meaning that it's okay to let things get out of balance once in a while, as long as you get back on track pretty quickly.

Bigs definitely stayed on track at Lilly. To say the pharmaceutical business is a complicated industry is like saying New York City has a few tall buildings. In his position, he was right in the middle of it and showed a knack for navigating those complexities to broker agreements among people who were extremely reluctant to come to the table. One of his admirers said that skill helped launch drugs that changed the practice of medicine forever.

Around 2006, Bigs embarked on what may have been his most challenging and far-reaching expedition into professional leadership, one that had enormous, national implications.

He had become increasingly concerned about the public's distrust of pharmaceutical companies' relationships with physicians. For years, those companies would compensate physicians in a number of ways, including free meals, consulting and speaking fees, even direct funding of research. Both sides kept those payments confidential for the most part.

Surveys showed that up to 94 percent of physicians had some financial interactions with the makers of drugs, devices, medical supplies, and similar products. Most of those interactions were meals, but US Senate investigations also found that prominent researchers at several institutions failed to report millions of dollars of outside compensation from drug makers. Other research showed that the drug maker–physician relationship influenced doctors in writing prescriptions. The situation was drawing media attention and fire. It became a contentious debate.

Bigs waded right into the roiling water–I guess he was ready to eat a big, ugly frog—with the goal of making Lilly a leading voice of integrity.

His solution was straightforward transparency. Bigs suggested to Lilly executives that the company disclose all grants and payments to physicians. As you might imagine, he faced more than a little resistance. But he also saw where the national debate was heading and had a strong moral compass about where Lilly should be in that debate. Those who hadn't already known him found out soon enough that Bigs was one very smart, very persuasive guy.

In September 2008, Lilly announced that it would post online all its payments to doctors for speaking and consulting services, starting in 2009. Later on, the same day of Lilly's announcement, another pharmaceutical giant, Merck & Co., stated it would disclose speaking fees paid to doctors.

About the same time he was working on the issue internally at Lilly, Bigs began sitting down with federal lawmakers to hammer out a comprehensive national policy on disclosing the compensation. He helped pull together the elements of what would become the Physician Payments Sunshine Act and made sure Lilly was the first pharmaceutical company to endorse the proposed legislation. He also made sure that the company's ideas were incorporated in the package.

A few months before Lilly's announcement at one of our Fionn MacCool Thursday night gatherings, Bigs mentioned that his back had been bothering him. He was a healthy, active guy, and we all agreed with his assessment that he'd thrown out his back playing basketball or engaging in some other activity that was too rigorous for someone approaching 41 years old. But the pain wasn't subsiding. We urged him to have it checked out.

Blood work pointed to liver abnormalities. Bigs went through more tests. For weeks, doctors were unable to pin down the source of the pain, which was intensifying. At the same time, the two of us were coaching Maggie and Nicolette and their team, having a ball as usual. We'd started indoor practices and were getting ready to get outside finally, another reason the coaches and girls were excited.

Finally, one of the tests Bigs took revealed a blockage at the head of his pancreas in the common bile duct. After doing his research, he decided to undergo several hours of a procedure that would remove the blockage and yield a precise diagnosis.

The night before the procedure, he invited the Fionn MacCool gang to hang out with him at home. When we were leaving, he hugged us like he always did and said he loved us like he always did. But this time, he walked out to the porch with us and, when we got in our cars, stood there waving while we pulled away. I remember thinking Bigs was worried, that maybe he knew something.

The next day, about 35 people packed the waiting room. When the lead surgeon came out after only a couple of hours, Brian Bigelow knew the reason was foreboding. The surgeon called about 15 family members into a separate room and gave them Bigs' diagnosis: stage 4 pancreatic cancer. He was told the average survival with stage 4 was six months and that patients had a 3 percent chance to beat it.

Who could know what exactly was going through Bigs' heart and mind when he was told? My guess is that although he was smart enough to have understood that pancreatic cancer was a possibility going into the procedure and knew that the diagnosis likely was a rapid, painful death sentence, the diagnosis probably was overwhelming and impossible to put into words. It not only was heartbreaking but confounding. At about 6 feet tall and 170 pounds,

Bigs was in good shape, a non-smoker, and had no family history of pancreatic cancer.

Yet, faced with all that, Bigs and his family chose to believe and hope he was in that slim 3 percent of the population. And, from somewhere inside him, Bigs summoned extraordinary courage.

Being around him then, all of us got to witness and learn from a unique example of leadership, day in and day out: how to live when you're dying. What priorities one should have. It distilled leadership and life to their most fundamental elements, and it was beautiful to watch that ultimate form of courage.

Bigs was fond of saying that there was always somebody who had it worse off and, "We're going to be all right. Everything's going to be all right."

I don't think he said those as a way of declaring that he would beat cancer, although he fought fiercely and with great hope. Bigs said those things as a way of reassuring others that everything was going to be all right regardless of the outcome. If he didn't make it, his family would survive and move forward. They would go on to have rewarding, full lives. He didn't want them to be fearful.

It's about as noble an approach as I could imagine. While he was dying a painful death—and, by the way, he never let people see how excruciating it got—Bigs made it a priority to reassure others that things were going to be okay.

His fight reflected that perspective in what I might call a fierce, calm resignation to live a normal life. Kris had deep enough character to adopt the same outlook.

"I was there to help Mike live," she told me, "not to help him die. He never gave up hope, which resulted in none of us ever giving up hope, either."

Brian found a new treatment that helped keep his big brother pain free for months. That enabled Bigs to keep going to work at Lilly and make progress on the physician payment disclosure effort. It also allowed him to continue engaging in one of his passions, traveling with his family. Before receiving the diagnosis, he had planned a family summer vacation to Yosemite and Napa Valley. They went. A few months later, the family traveled to the Smoky Mountains over a fall break. He even kept playing golf when the pain wasn't too intense.

He was losing weight, losing his hair, and enduring the painful contradiction of chemotherapy—that the treatment can ravage the body as badly as the disease. Still, he kept coming to most practices and all our games. Some days, Bigs was so sick, he'd excuse himself from the field, walk in the woods to vomit, then come right back to practice. Other times, he'd sit in a lawn chair on an 80-degree day, shivering under layers of blankets.

He was there in part because he loved those girls that much. When so much of his day was filled with pain, the girls personified pure joy. He wanted to drink up all that and gain strength and energy from it.

I believe he had other reasons for being there. Bigs was one of those people who had the wisdom of an old soul. My guess is that, again, he knew showing up had more to do with others than it did with him. He certainly wanted to allay the girls' concerns. By seeing him as often as they did—even though it was so sad to watch his decline—they took away lessons that had nothing to do with playing a game and everything to do with growing as human beings. They saw that real bravery can look different in different people at different times. They discovered that they could be extremely sad and extremely courageous at the same time, which gave them a higher degree of reassurance. They learned that they could face this awful set of circumstances or similar challenges down the road in their lives and survive.

His presence was inspirational and beautiful and made me realize that you don't have to be a championship soccer team to learn great lessons on leadership and life. You can learn those on a team of little girls in a recreational league in suburban Indianapolis.

The girls responded with the genuine, astonishing grace of children. They embraced Bigs, never wavering in their love and respect for him. Almost as important, they embraced each other, helping each other get through. Our team did well that fall, making it to the championship game, but losing in what would be Bigs' final game as coach.

His presence at our soccer practices and games also underscored that his most effective therapy, his best medicine, was being surrounded by people. It probably took his mind off the pain. And, it was more indicative of his core. Remember, Bigs loved people. The illness didn't change that or anything else about him. It didn't bring forth a new Mike Bigelow. It just deepened and reinforced the one I loved.

Like many of his closest friends, I stopped by his house almost every day. He and I set aside Tuesday mornings about 10 o'clock specifically as our days to take a little walk when he could handle it. We'd usually go through his neighborhood, pass nearby woods, and end at a golf course. On days when he couldn't handle a walk, he wouldn't make a big deal about it. He'd simply say it wasn't a good day for him, and we'd hang out at home and chat.

Whether at home or on our walks, he'd talk only briefly about what he was going through and only if I asked. Then he'd be very matter of fact: Everything tasted like metal; he couldn't hold a cold can of Coke because his fingertips were so temperature sensitive. I knew on some of those days he was in total agony, but Bigs refused to go there, instead moving the conversation to other topics, often about me.

One of his favorite subjects was the story of my college soccer experience. He loved hearing about it and kept saying what a wonderfully inspiring story it was, how it would make a great book and movie and that I needed to make that happen. That was Bigs, always pushing and encouraging me to go further than I thought possible. I listened to his encouragement. Five years later, my story became the book, *To Chase a Dream.*

Bigs did that with everyone who visited him—made them feel like they were more important than himself and what he was experiencing. The result was that visitors always would leave feeling better than when they'd arrived. It was a poignant, rare demonstration of selflessness and generosity, and, like I said, it was very true to who he was before and during his illness.

By late winter, Bigs had survived nearly two times longer than expected, and he'd done so with gusto and a generous spirit. In early March, he even traveled back and forth to Washington, DC, to share his expertise on the physician payment issue at the First National Disclosure Summit. He'd become a leading legal expert on the subject.

At the same time, his condition had deteriorated severely. Doctors told him they'd done everything they could do. Kris was adamant about not losing hope, not giving up. Bigs said he wanted to keep fighting, too, but he shared with her that his body was moving quickly toward complete shutdown. It simply couldn't fight any longer.

Still committed to keeping normalcy in their lives and wanting to enjoy one of his family's favorite activities, travel, the Bigelows, along with Mike's parents, took a plane to Naples, Florida, for spring break. They got a little sunshine and watched the NCAA men's basketball Final Four on TV. Bigs ate his favorite meal, veal pappardelle, at his favorite restaurant, Campiello, on Saturday. By Saturday night, his condition had become acute. For the first time since his diagnosis, he was agitated, unsure of where he was. The family got home to Fishers by Monday night. The pain was so excruciating that Mike slept in a family room recliner. His family slept on the floor around him.

The next morning on my way to a meeting, Kris called and told me I better get to their house quick. I arrived shortly before 11 and found him sitting in the recliner, barely breathing, and unable to acknowledge me or any of the other 30 or so people gathered around him. Kris was right. These were his final hours. Hospice arrived. Kris, Kate, Maggie, and Matt held Bigs' hands, trying to comfort him as much as possible while they wept.

About 2:30 p.m., Kris and the kids whispered to Bigs that it was okay for him to go, that they would be all right, and Bigs took his last breath. That's what he was waiting for—his family to confirm they were going to be okay. Then, finally, he would leave.

In that instant, through overwhelming heartbreak, I swear I saw something tangible and extraordinary happen. Bigs' fierce optimism, energy, and peace flowed from him to Kris and the kids. Maybe everyone in the room caught a little slice of it, at least I hope so.

Over the next few minutes, each of us in the room took a moment to say goodbye to him. All I remember is that I couldn't stop sobbing. After a while, funeral home staff arrived to take Bigs' body.

It probably comes as no surprise that people waited two hours in line at the wake to pay their respects or that a couple thousand people showed up for Bigs' funeral, many cutting short their spring break trips to return.

After the funeral, a bunch of us returned to the house where many others passed through to pay their respects and celebrate Bigs' life. We served two of Bigs' favorites: wine from Napa and craft beef. We told a lot of Bigs' stories, and we laughed. Something like compassionate electricity flowed throughout the house, which is another way of saying Bigs was right there with us. And, when we five Fionn MacCool guys left, we hugged each other and said, "I love you." We do that to this day.

The next morning, I woke and felt a heavy, unshakeable sadness, an aimless and empty helplessness. I called Kris and met the family for breakfast. I kept saying that we needed to do something to maintain Bigs' memory, and we came up with the idea of a golf outing. The next day, I got on the phone with Mark Wright, who immediately agreed to help organize it.

A week after he passed, Lilly awarded Bigs the prestigious Chairman's Ovation Award, citing his "tireless efforts to build public trust and confidence in the relationships between our industry and physicians."

Three months later, we held the first Bigelow Open. Since then, the annual outing has been nothing too fancy—Bigs would like that—yet raised more than half a million dollars for pancreatic cancer research. I think it would be almost as important, from Bigs' perspective, to know that every time a new person attends, he or she tells us it feels like a family reunion.

If you're interested in learning more, check us out here www.pancyst. org.

A year after Bigs passed, the Physician Payment Sunshine Act proposal became law. It requires makers of medical products, such as pharmaceutical companies, to disclose payments or other transfers of value made to physicians or teaching hospitals. It also calls for certain manufacturers and other organizations to report physician ownership or investments in those entities.

In 2016, Bigs received the Lilly Legal Legacy Award for individuals who "will be forever remembered for their legal contributions and commitments to the values of integrity, excellence, and respect for people." Lilly's general counsel said Bigs was "a clarion call for hope, passion, and integrity" and still is.

Every once in a while, I think about his effort to bring more integrity to medicine while he was fighting for his life, and I marvel at his sheer strength, stamina, and selflessness. I also think here was a guy who played such an important leadership role in making life better for perhaps millions of people and yet so few know his name. Maybe that's the way Bigs would like it.

The season after he passed, I was coaching two teams—the girls team he and I ran and my son Trey's team. The girls wore black armbands to mourn and honor Bigs. Into the coaching void stepped Jimmy Vuotto, whose daughter Elle was on the team. Not only was Jimmy spirited, fun, and knowledgeable, he became my rock, able to appreciate how much I grieved for Bigs and still helped me push forward. It was a precarious position to be in, and Jimmy had the perfect disposition for it.

That year, the league organized things a little differently, staging the championship tournament at the start of the season instead of at the end. We got in the tournament, and the girls decided to dedicate their performance to Bigs.

We ended up in the final again, just like we had for Bigs' last game. As luck would have it, so did Trey's team. Both games were played back to back on the same field; girls first. Because I coached both teams, they became informal cheerleading squads for each other. It was a pretty cool dynamic.

In the championship match, the girls focused like I'd never seen them before, scrappier than ever. It was a really, really tough game.

Regulation ended in a tie. After playing overtime, the score remained tied, and we won on penalty kicks.

Some coaches may have viewed that kind of win as nothing more than a fun game for a bunch of 10-year-old girls. But that victory was one of the most rewarding of my life. The joy on their faces that shone through the tears all of us shed was unlike anything I've experienced.

While the girls, Jimmy, and I were celebrating on the field, the boys started to warm up a few feet away. Luke, one of my players, jogged up to me and held out a Rosary. I recognized that it was from Medjugorje, a site in Bosnia and Herzegovina that is associated with miracles. Since the 1980s, thousands have made pilgrimages there to view apparitions of Virgin Mary.

"Is this your Rosary, coach?" he asked.

It wasn't. I'd never seen it before.

"Well, it was in the grass next to you during the game," Luke said.

I looked at him then looked at the Rosary again. Something caught in my throat. I held out my hand.

"I'll take it, Luke," I said. "Thanks."

We have the freedom to believe what we want to believe. Some might think it was coincidence that a Rosary was next to me while I coached that game, that it accidentally slipped out of a kid's bag or a woman's purse or a man's coat pocket while they walked by that exact spot.

That's not what I believe.

I slipped the Rosary into my pocket. That's where it is today, where it's been every day since that game, since Bigs helped me coach and inspired the girls to give their best for each other.

I take it out every single day and say a little prayer, knowing that Bigs is standing next to me, a friend who was the epitome of leadership, mentoring me and countless others. I suspect he'll do that for the rest of our lives. He lived the values of integrity, hope, presence, humor, authenticity, gratitude, competitiveness, and, most of all, caring, to his last breath. He lived a life of *philotimo* leadership.

Just like they assured Bigs, his family is doing all right. He's left a void in their lives that is impossible to fill but also gave them everything a father could.

Kris has done a remarkable job raising their three children and carrying on as a strong link in all the relationships Bigs and she built over the years.

I read a story in the local press about Bigs and thought what Kris said captured their journey so well.

"I think what you learn is that even though God doesn't answer the prayers exactly as you want them," Kris told the Carmel Community Newsletter, "there is still good. We're here, and the kids are doing really great, and even though Mike isn't physically here, he is here in so many ways."

The kids *are* doing really great. Kate is a junior at Indiana University where she's studying pre-med. Maggie is set to start nursing school at Purdue University in the fall of 2017, and Matt is a sophomore at Cathedral High School where he's on the golf team. That's also where I coach the boys' varsity soccer team and where I persuaded Matt to be team manager this season. I could use another Bigelow on the sidelines with me.

And, this may come as a surprise, but Bigs still travels extensively. After his cremation, Kris kept the urn of some of his ashes at home.

Every time one of his friends or relatives is getting ready to travel someplace adventurous, beautiful, or fun, she tells them to stop by the house and then gives them some of Bigs' ashes.

We've sprinkled Bigs on some of his favorite places: the grass at Wrigley Field and on Lucas Oil Stadium's turf, in Napa Valley, in tee boxes at a variety of golf courses, even at his favorite restaurant in Naples, Florida. We've also hit a few other places that we'll keep to ourselves. And, we'll continue spreading them. We know he's enjoying the adventure.

And, we figure the more of Bigs we spread around this world, the better.

# EPILOGUE: DISTILLING THE CODE

Like I said at the outset, this book is a somewhat unconventional look at leadership, and it all centers around the concept of *philotimo*, the Greek word that, roughly translated, means possessing a deliberate and conscious honor in doing the right thing, an honor that is not ego-driven or showy, but more of a quiet confidence. The words on the little chalkboard in my parents' kitchen distill it best in an excerpt from Philippians 2: 3-4:

"Do nothing out of selfish ambition or vain conceit. Rather, in humility value others above yourselves, not looking to your own interests but each of you to the interests of others."

I might add, "getting more joy out of the success of others, than you do from your own successes" to the board if there was enough room.

My parents emphasized those concepts with all of us five kids in small and big ways, like making sure our whole crew attended each other's activities, and they made sure never to compare us with one another. They always encouraged us but also were honest with us. Kindness to each other was another emphasis our parents created in the family.

All those lessons taught us to be leaders no matter where we were in the family, youngest or oldest, boy or girl. That's one of the central themes of this book: You don't have to be in a traditional leadership position to be a leader. That role exists across all levels of our society and culture. In other words, it doesn't matter what place you occupy. What matters is how you occupy that space.

And leadership has to be a conscious decision by the individual. You have to commit to being someone who cares most about overall results and team strength rather than individual success; someone who cares deeply about leaving a place in much better shape than when you arrived. And, someone willing to learn and grow into the position.

I was blessed from the moment I was born by the examples my parents set. They weren't interested in dictating as much as really listening and supporting, helping us make decisions and determine the path that was best. They were transparent.

I realized that leadership starts as a kid with the decision to be responsible to others in the family, to build trust by being unafraid to share your feelings and trusting others in your family to help get you where you want to go, and by engaging yourself in your siblings' and parents' own fears and struggles and triumphs.

And, my parents showed us that leadership is generosity, too. Throughout our moves all over the Midwest, they'd always immerse themselves in the community, work to change things for the better, and share whatever expertise they had with others.

I liked my youngest brother Dino's observation as a summary of my parents' approach when he gave me his definition of leadership over breakfast one Father's Day morning:

"One, a leader gives people something to belong to," Dino said. "Second, a leader will provide a clear direction or clear vision, and third, that leader will inspire others to bring out the best."

I think Dino did such a nice job distilling leadership. I also think that perspective takes time and life experiences to attain.

****

When I decided at the last minute to try out for Indiana University's powerhouse men's soccer team, I was embarking on a lengthy, arduous, and very indirect journey to learn the observations Dino made. But it was worth it.

It started with me as the guy who worked his rear end off to barely make the team as a practice dummy, only to have coaches repeatedly tell me I'd never play and suggest that I transfer. Then came the injury that derailed my dream of playing for the best college team in the country for an entire season and nearly killed my career altogether.

I hung in there and tried my best to keep an optimistic outlook and learn from leaders I respected. My fifth year in the program, through a set of circumstances that no one probably could have predicted, I found myself captain of the once-proud soccer team that had become decimated generally because of a lack of leadership that had deteriorated and was deeply flawed.

I leaned on what I'd learned over the years at IU—constructive and destructive—and in my own upbringing. Then, in my final season, I did my best to lead a group of unranked unknowns. The result was an unprecedented, 16-game winning streak to become the number-one ranked college team in the nation.

It was a pretty extraordinary experience, one that you can read about in my previous book, *To Chase a Dream*. That journey helped me immensely in dealing with all sorts of adversity that would come later in my life, and it helped me compose a few principles that I try to live by in leadership, in life, and in professional and personal roles.

First, set attainable goals that are a real stretch. Write them down. Write down why you want to get there and exactly how you're going to get there. Place them someplace where you'll see them every day and think about saying a little affirmative prayer every day. Don't worry too much about how or when you want to reach the goal. Just make sure you're moving in the right direction, and you'll get there, or at least pretty darn close.

Second, have pie-in-the-sky dreams: president of the United States, hitting a home run in the World Series, playing lead guitar in front of thousands of fans, winning a Nobel Prize or Academy Award. Regularly picture yourself in the position of achieving that dream and enjoy the sensation. You've planted the seed and, probably, the desire to nurture that seed. Who knows? It could grow into something really cool. Help let it happen.

Third, surround yourself with supportive, enthusiastic, can-do people as friends and mentors. Be one of those people and don't be surprised if all that positive energy comes right back at you.

Fourth, believe in yourself and know that you can achieve what you want. Weave a peaceful mind with incredible desire and hard work.

Fifth, persevere and embrace the journey even if it doesn't end where you wanted. Be willing to endure the rough patches and know that failure is a better learning and growing experience than success. When you do fail, absorb the lesson, adapt, and move forward. Don't beat yourself up. Patient persistence is the key. Humor, especially the ability to laugh at yourself, is vital.

Finally, rely on your faith. Prayer is powerful energy that heals, comforts, inspires, and gives courage. When you've done all that you can, relinquish control to God and rely on your faith. The sooner you can place that trust in God, the sooner you will walk through life with more abundance, surer footing, a calmer mind, and a loving heart.

****

My college soccer experience included the strong formative presence of IU coach, Jerry Yeagley, who didn't start out being my biggest supporter but came to be. Coaches play powerful roles in any athlete's life, and I certainly have paid close attention to how they do their jobs for effective tips I can borrow and ineffective ones that I want to avoid.

When I reconnected with Coach Yeagley during various events organized around *To Chase a Dream,* and I made a point of sitting down with him, I got to hear more about his own leadership journey and philosophy he achieved by going through that journey.

Like every coach, Coach Yeagley took his experiences with coaches while he was a player and applied them—or deliberately didn't—when he became a coach. In his case, he had two distinctly different coaches. One was a highly detailed, aggressive guy who motivated through negative reinforcement and fear; the other was much more compassionate and humanistic. He passed along his passion for a game he thought was beautiful.

Coach Yeagley's own overall approach to leadership tended toward the more humanistic approach and boiled down to knowing your objectives, having a plan to achieve those goals, and believing in yourself and what you're doing. His belief that leaders should be fiercely competitive also included the notion that a leader should be unafraid to be challenged and should welcome strong people around him or her.

Leaders must adapt, Coach Yeagley said. He was big on emphasizing the positive traits of his players and creating a family atmosphere that built a strong bond. He had a strong passion for what he was doing.

In the end, a great deal of leadership had to do with the psychological, specifically with finding the way to get a person to self-motivate, he said. Coach Yeagley is a firm believer in performance following attitude, good or bad.

"My approach is you have to achieve excellence through performance ignited by motivation," he told me while we sat at a Steak 'n Shake. "Like Vince Lombardi said, 'Perfection is unachievable, but if you chase it hard enough, you just might find excellence.' I strove for excellence, and motivation is crucial."

When he saw his student-athletes take ownership of their performance, holding each other accountable on and off the field, that's when he knew he'd gotten the leadership thing right.

At the base of it all, the foundation of what he was as a leader was trust. Again and again that word would come up during all my conversations with leaders when they would talk about getting the absolute best out of their people. Coach Yeagley said it started with being genuine with his players. Others said it was transparency and honesty.

One coach who had that mastered was Coach Mike Krzyzewski, leader of Duke University men's basketball team, a perennial contender for the national championship.

When I had a chance to observe Coach K at work for a few days, what I saw was someone who made a very definitive point to show his players how much he cared about each and every one of them. I saw it right away when he'd hug each one as they got off the bus as they arrived at Lucas Oil Stadium for the 2010 Final Four. And, I could tell by the practices—the precision and intensity and purpose but also the looseness and confidence, the fun—that he was getting the most out of his players.

In those five days, I saw up close a man who was incredibly focused on the moment, respectful, and consistent to everyone, even to me, a lowly volunteer who'd been assigned to his team as a liaison between them and the host, Indiana Sports Corp. That's how you build trust and integrity, and it has paid off in his teams' five national championships, his six gold medals leading the USA Men's National Team, and an astonishing overall record of 1,043 wins and 321 losses going into the 2016-17 season.

Duke got one of its national championships the year I hung out with the team, and I'd established a nice rapport with Coach K in our brief time together. After the final, he accepted the trophy, did the interviews, cut down his piece of the net, and went into the locker room with his players. A few minutes later, he emerged with a national championship cap for me. A few weeks after that, he mailed a personal note thanking me again for my service to the team.

That's a guy who understands that all great leaders must have the human connection in relationships. It demonstrates a man with a deep understanding of leadership through *philotimo*.

In my own modest coaching activities, I've stressed many of the things you read about: getting the players to believe in themselves and in each other; working hard; and having unity, trust, and optimism. But I may have stumbled on my strongest team-building asset by starting "Reflection Monday" with my youngest daughter's club team. We would spend the first 15 to 20 minutes of practice every Monday talking about life, about the past weekend, school, the girls' social life, their successes, challenges, and their dreams. We talked about everything except soccer.

Over the years, that team built a bond that was incredibly strong, built through transparency, open communication, and trust. It worked on the field and off. They learned to empathize and love each other. It opened their eyes, minds, and hearts.

And the results transferred to our performance. Our first year, we were ranked 54th in the state. Our third year we won the Indiana State Championship.

We built something bigger than success in a game, though. And, when I run into those girls now and we chat, they'll tell me how much they enjoyed the team. They almost never say anything about the championship. I think they realized their experience was about something much more valuable.

****

In the rollercoaster ride that was Soccer Unlimited, think I learned an enormous amount about leadership and life, starting with a strong focus on personal relationships based on trust, hard work, simply treating people well, and most important, transparency. Those characteristics in how I ran the business helped immensely when building it and when things started collapsing.

That transparency piece was really valuable when it came to leading my family through the rough times. Instead of trying to pretend I was invincible and closing myself off to our children, which would have confused and hurt them, Sherri and I made the difficult decision to share with them what had happened, always with the assurance that things would be okay. Our children responded heroically.

Also, I really tested the concept that, as a leader, you have to be resilient and believe in yourself and determine who you are, what your priorities are, and why you do what you do. The ordeal reinforced gratitude as a key component of my life—gratitude for all those who were generous to me, mostly Sherri, the kids, and other members of my family, close friends, and customers who genuinely kept supporting me.

And, as trying as that experience was, I have never for a second regretted getting involved with my family business. I may have done a few things differently now that I have the wisdom of experience, but what happened is what happened, and I look back on that journey with powerful memories and lessons learned, perhaps the most important being the value of sharing around the kitchen table. In the end, the journey made me much stronger, wiser, and more sincere about what and who really matter to me, and it deepened my relationships with the people who matter most.

****

One of the things that really matters to me is the community, and being active in the community always has been a large part of my leadership code. I learned it from my parents, who set a terrific example.

And, when I think about my relationship with Allison Melangton, I witnessed how her sense of leadership expands the concept of community and makes community so integral to leadership. Her example as CEO and president of the Super Bowl XLVI Host Committee shed light on a person who might not fit the stereotypical leadership profile and who approaches the role in an innovative way that leads to a remarkably successful outcome.

Allison is a deeply spiritual person—it's the "why" of who she is and her leadership philosophy—and she'd lost sight of that early in her tenure running the Super Bowl. Once she found it again, she was able to handle the enormous stress of the job. It's a great lesson, I think, in determining purpose in our lives, and discovering that once the purpose or the "why" is clear, things start to come together in the ways we'd hoped—sometimes in even better ways.

When she told me the Super Bowl was not about what happens on the field, even though most of the world thinks that's what it's about, I had an ah-ha moment. Her fundamental approach to her very pressure-packed role was to make this Super Bowl about engaging the community in ways that made Indianapolis and the rest of Indiana a better place—not just with one huge injection of revenue, but in ways that brought the community closer to establish enduring change. She focused on changing people's lives, creating great moments of connectedness, making people feel valued, and, in general, making a positive impact. Every idea that came her way had to meet the same, overarching criteria: It had to change the city for the better, or it wasn't going to be included.

A key part of that strategy was that Allison directed her group to talk with everybody who reached out to them, whether they had an idea or just wanted to help. That approach built what Allison called "a groundswell of support for us," a trust throughout the community.

Allison reinforced that by establishing a collaborative leadership among her entire crew, which may have gone against conventional wisdom when it came to Super Bowls and similar events, but she knew exactly what she was doing.

At the heart of her leadership philosophy were those two words I heard a lot during my conversations: transparency and trust. In her case, they come from hard work, honesty, daily contact, communication, and a culture that promotes all that. Her emphasis in fostering that atmosphere was to talk often with a lot of people.

She took the flood of volunteers and formed 62 leadership committees, about four times more than the number for any previous Super Bowl. A total of 160 leaders were in charge of those committees, and those leaders committed to working in the community for three years. She used the entire network in part to engage and train the next generation of civic and community leaders.

The results of Allison's leadership were very tangible: A volunteer force of 8,000 people helped make the Indianapolis Super Bowl of 2012 the most engaging and successfully organized Super Bowl in history. On the financial side, through the Super Bowl Legacy Initiative, nearly $154 million in federal, state, local, business, foundational, and private investment was made in Indianapolis' struggling Near Eastside neighborhood.

A variety of green initiatives led to more than 1 million pounds of carbon and 2.5 million gallons of water conserved, the planting of nearly 3,000 trees, the collection of 21 tons of electronics for recycling, and recovery of 46,000 pounds of food from Super Bowl events that were distributed to those in need. A total of 46 large, vivid murals were painted in public places. In another one of Allison's promotions, women donated 700 healthy breast tissue samples to the Susan G. Komen for the Cure Tissue Bank at the Indiana University Simon Cancer Center, which collects blood samples, breast tissue, and saliva for researchers all over the world. In addition, various events raised $1 million for the bank.

But perhaps her most innovative idea was Super Scarves in which people knitted scarves for and wrote personal notes to the volunteers at the Super Bowl. It was a huge hit. More than 13,000 people from 45 states, Washington, DC, and England, Canada, South Africa, and Belgium made scarves.

That leadership experience was an invaluable one for Allison, and it prompted me to ask about what were the most formative experiences in her own leadership journey.

Great mentors were one. People with transparency, vision, and sometimes brutal but loving honesty in dealing with her have inspired her to create great leaders from younger people.

\*\*\*\*

What can I say about Mike Bigelow?

I occasionally think about how serendipity, fate, or God brought us together through something as random as our daughters being in the same kindergarten class. And, I have to chuckle that the guy who started our relationship by being my assistant soccer coach for a bunch of five-year-old girls became such an inspirational mentor to me.

Although our relationship got off to a humorously rocky start, we became fast friends—so fast in fact that we set aside one Thursday a month to have a couple beers and talk at a local watering hole. Our group gradually expanded to six guys. Among the things all of us loved about Bigs was that he always wanted to take the conversation someplace more meaningful. He loved being surrounded by people, and he was authentic about engaging others. All of us cherished those evenings, which Bigs would conclude by giving each of us a hug and telling each guy he loved them.

As a coach, he was able to push our players to do more than I think they thought they could, but in constructive and encouraging ways that always promoted the broader interests of the team first. He had a similar effect on our friendship, pushing me to do more than I thought I could, offering advice, and always encouraging me.

As assistant general counsel at the pharmaceutical giant Eli Lilly, Bigs took on a complex leadership role in his professional life, too. At its core was integrity.

He became concerned about a long-time, widespread practice of pharmaceutical companies compensating doctors in ways that generally were kept confidential but that also might have influenced doctors when they wrote prescriptions. His solution was to suggest that Lilly disclose its payments to doctors and, on a larger scale, to work with federal policymakers on national legislation that would require compensation.

After navigating a fair amount of resistance, Bigs succeeded in both efforts.

In accomplishing those achievements, Bigs displayed many traits of a great leader: integrity, persuasion, and inspiration to do the right thing for the greater good. The results benefitted perhaps millions of people.

A few months before he turned 41, Bigs received shocking and heartbreaking news: a diagnosis of stage 4 pancreatic cancer. He was given six months to live. How my close friend responded to that diagnosis ended up being the most powerful leadership example of my life.

Bigs fought fiercely and with great hope and essentially became more of what I loved about him. He committed to a life of normalcy, continuing his important work on the physicians' compensation issue, attending nearly all our soccer practices and games, even playing golf as much as possible and taking his family on vacations—all through excruciating pain. He also surrounded himself with people. Throughout the ordeal, Bigs made it a priority to reassure others that things were going to be okay, no matter what.

His approach was sad and beautiful and provided invaluable lessons about true bravery and empathy.

He ended up surviving nearly two times longer than expected, and he'd done so with gusto and a generous spirit. When he passed in March 2009, surrounded by dozens of relatives and friends in his home, I saw Bigs' fierce optimism, energy, and peace flow from him to Kris and the kids, and perhaps to everyone in the room.

Every once in a while, I think about Bigs' effort to bring more integrity to medicine while he was fighting for his life, carrying on as normally as possible and making sure his family was okay. I marvel at his sheer strength, stamina, and selflessness. I also think about the guy who played such an important leadership role in making life better for perhaps of millions of people and yet so few know his name. Maybe that's the way Bigs would have liked it.

Bigs' friends kept his memory alive by building an enduring legacy through an annual golf outing, the Bigelow Open. Since our first one in 2009, the open has raised more than half a million dollars for pancreatic cancer research. Many who attend say it has the feel of a family reunion, which I think would have made Bigs beam with energy.

****

When I look at all that has come my way—good and bad, challenging and smooth, discouraging and uplifting—I think, in the end, I'm grateful. I'm grateful for all of it, as hard and heartbreaking as some of it has been, because I believe all these experiences helped me.

They helped inspire me, strengthen me, helped me realize the right way to do things and the wrong way. They helped me figure out who I am and what's important to me, helped me walk with God, helped me forgive. I've learned the value and skill of hard work; that life isn't always fair but that you persevere and keep plugging away as best you can; and, that when we lose someone we love, we must make it our mission to perpetuate their goodness.

I've learned that we all have the strength and skill to accomplish remarkable things, if we are committed to being present at all times, and that things will get better. I guess that's another way to say that this journey has helped my optimism and hope.

I've learned that you don't need a big stage or big title to be a leader—that leadership starts from within and must be committed to on a daily basis. I've learned the value of relationships and the gift of listening as a powerful form of communication.

I'll never get it exactly right. I'll never be the perfect leader. That's okay. We're all constantly evolving, which is healthy and makes the journey so fascinating. I will continue to fail, which is okay, too. Failure might, in fact, be the best teacher. If nothing else, it certainly keeps us humble.

When I throw all those things in a basket and toss them a little and then let them settle, what I come up with is what I mentioned at the outset of this book: *philotimo*. This journey and all its struggles and triumphs, grind, and grace has helped my sense of *philotimo*. The journey also reinforced my appreciation and love for sitting around the kitchen table.

Now I hope, no matter where you are in life and what position you hold in a family, business, or other entity, you see how you can be a leader and why I'm so grateful for all that my leadership journey has given me. Maybe you can find gratitude in your journey, too. It's all about attitude, perspective, and hard work, and those are totally up to you.

# ■ CREDITS

**Cover Design:** Sannah Inderelst

**Interior Design:** Eva Feldmann

**Layout:** zerosoft

**Managing Editor:** Elizabeth Evans

# MORE GREAT TITLES

# FROM MEYER & MEYER SPORT

**MEYER & MEYER Sport**
Von-Coels-Str. 390
52080 Aachen
Germany

Phone    +49 02 41 - 9 58 10 - 13
Fax    +49 02 41 - 9 58 10 - 10
E-Mail    sales@m-m-sports.com
E-Books    www.m-m-sports.com

**MEYER & MEYER SPORT**

All books available as E-books.